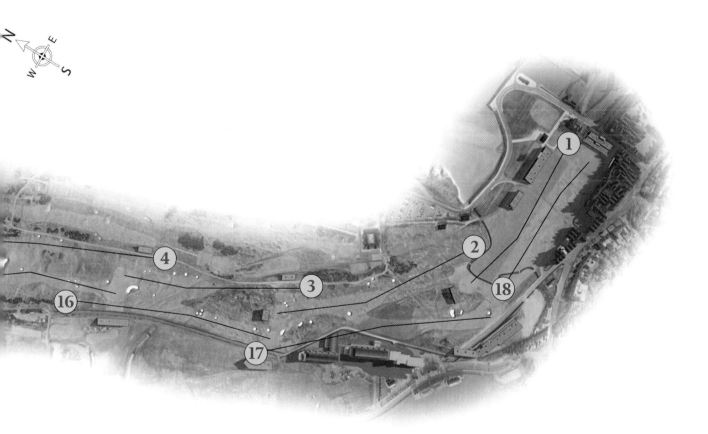

# THE OPEN

## 144TH ST ANDREWS

Aurum Press

Aurum Press
74-77 White Lion Street, London N1 9PF

Published 2015 by Aurum Press

Copyright 2015 R&A Championships Limited

Course illustration by Strokesaver

Project coordinator: Sarah Wooldridge
Additional thanks to NTT Data

A CIP catalogue record for this book is available
from the British Library

ISBN-13: 978 1 78131 524 8

Designed and produced by Davis Design
Colour retouching by Luciano Retouching Services, Inc.
Printed in Slovenia by Svet Print d.o.o.

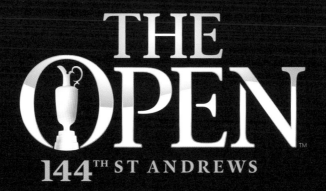

# THE OPEN

## 144TH ST ANDREWS

**EDITOR**
Andy Farrell

## WRITERS AND PHOTOGRAPHERS

| Writers | Getty Images | The R&A | Golf Editors |
|---|---|---|---|
| Peter Dixon | Andrew Redington | Ross Kinnaird | Maxx Wolfson |
| Andy Farrell | Streeter Lecka | David Cannon | Steve Rose |
| John Hopkins | Stuart Franklin | Warren Little | Jaime Lawson |
| Lewine Mair | Matthew Lewis | Ian Walton | Mark Trowbridge |
| Art Spander | Mike Ehrmann | Richard Heathcote | Rob Harborne |
| Alistair Tait | | Mark Runnacles | |
| | | James Cheadle | |

# Foreword

*By Zach Johnson*

As I said at the presentation at St Andrews, I am honoured and humbled to be the Champion Golfer of the Year. Dreams were realised and goals accomplished that special week at the Home of Golf. I feel blessed to hold the precious Claret Jug and know it could easily have gone to so many other great champions, especially Louis Oosthuizen and Marc Leishman. Patience and perseverance were the keys to the week and making the best of my opportunities, particularly in the play-off.

It is still hard to put into words what it means to win at St Andrews, the birthplace of this great game and a venue that needs to be on the bucket list of all those who love the game. It may sound corny now I'm an Open Champion, but I have said many, many times this is the most fun golf Championship inside the ropes.

To Mr Dawson and The R&A, you host and showcase one of the best events in sport. It's an honour just to be invited to play, let alone to win. It was a testing week with the elements for everyone, but a tip of the cap must go to greenkeeping staff, who were all champions that week. And the fans were fantastic, their support is something I will always cherish.

There are so many people to thank for supporting me throughout my career but two stand out. One is my right-hand man Damon Green, my caddie. Golf is a team game and he is my partner. The other is my wife, Kim, who was there to share in my victory in Scotland and who I thank for all her support and belief. I had a peace about that day, it was divine, and for that I thank the Lord.

*Zach Johnson*

# The Championship Committee

**CHAIRMAN**

Peter Unsworth

**DEPUTY CHAIRMAN**

Clive Brown

**COMMITTEE**

| | |
|---|---|
| Stuart Allison | Nick Ellis |
| Peter Arthur | John Louden |
| Andrew Bathurst | Charlie Maran |
| David Boyle | David Meacher |
| Peter Cowell | Andrew Stracey |

**CHIEF EXECUTIVE**

Peter Dawson

**CHIEF EXECUTIVE DESIGNATE**

Martin Slumbers

**EXECUTIVE DIRECTOR – CHAMPIONSHIPS**

Johnnie Cole-Hamilton

**EXECUTIVE DIRECTOR – RULES AND EQUIPMENT STANDARDS**

David Rickman

# Introduction

*By Peter Unsworth*
*Chairman of the Championship Committee of The R&A*

The 144TH Open at St Andrews had all the ingredients of a great Championship: a worthy Champion, a dramatic finish and a leaderboard packed with the world's top players going into the back nine of the final round. Zach Johnson showed great composure and played tremendous golf to win the play-off with the defending St Andrews Champion Louis Oosthuizen and Australia's Marc Leishman. It was wonderful to see the Champion Golfer of the Year being so warmly greeted by the St Andrews galleries as he paraded the Claret Jug.

The Irish amateur Paul Dunne's performance in being tied for the lead after the third round was remarkable and the first time that has happened since Bobby Jones led going into the final round at St Andrews in 1927. It is testimony to the growing strength of the amateur game that he was one of five amateurs to make the cut with America's Jordan Niebrugge going on to win the Silver Medal.

The Champion Golfers' Challenge prior to the Championship was a true celebration of The Open and it was a joy to see Peter Thomson, Arnold Palmer, Gary Player and Tom Watson to the fore at such a historic gathering of Champions at the Home of Golf. It was also entirely fitting that Tom received such a warm reception from the galleries when he completed his final round in The Open on the 40th anniversary of his first appearance in the Championship.

There are so many people who play a part in delivering The Open and they all deserve huge credit. I would, in particular, like to thank the St Andrews Championship Committee and the staff at St Andrews Links Trust as well as the many hundreds of volunteers who worked hard throughout the week to ensure the smooth running of the Championship.

*Peter M.G. Unsworth*

# Beloved Watson takes a final bow

*Art Spander offers a personal appreciation of the five-time Champion.*

Darkness had all but closed in on the long Scottish summer evening, and figuratively on Tom Watson. You thought of the poet Dylan Thomas' words. But Watson was not raging against the dying of the light. He was embracing it, celebrating along with persistent, loyal and appreciative fans that as 10 o'clock approached were not going to miss this last, wonderful hurrah.

In golf there is no better place to finish, a round, a championship or a career, than the 18th at St Andrews, walking triumphantly down the wide fairway, stopping to pose and wave from the stones of the Swilcan Bridge, striding across Grannie Clark's Wynd, and

then soaking up the cheers and applause of those up on the balconies or down along The Links.

Forty years after his first Open, when he won in a play-off over Jack Newton at Carnoustie, Watson was playing his last. We thought of the passing of time and of torches, of a young man from the American Midwest with a shock of reddish brown hair and a gap in his front teeth who seemingly before our eyes had become 65, and no less importantly had become beloved.

Five Opens Tom Watson won, only one fewer than the record set by the brilliant Harry Vardon; five Opens and dozens of accolades, if not thousands.

None of those victories came on the Old Course, and he knew this ultimate Championship, battered by the wind and rain, wouldn't change much to his way of thinking or to ours. Icons do not need embellishment.

What golf always has needed, however, were individuals who not only played the game successfully, but honourably. From the time he was a student at Stanford University near San Francisco — no, from the time he was a boy in Kansas City — Watson grasped what was expected of him and what he expected from golf.

Watson's son Michael, 33, carried the bag at St Andrews, and as the two of them, pro and caddie, father and son, came down the 18th, trying to complete a second round that because of the weather for many would carry over to another day, Watson said, "Michael there should be no tears. This should be all joy." Which it was for everyone.

Although he never finished first in an Open at St Andrews, coming in second to Severiano Ballesteros in 1984 after running afoul of the Road Hole — as have so many others, including Jordan Spieth this year — Watson said he thought of the story of Bobby Jones, who did win an Open at St Andrews in 1927, returning to the Old Course a few years after his 1930 Grand Slam to play a friendly game.

"I'm not putting myself in the same shoes as Bobby Jones," said Watson, "but walking up the 18th, as the legend goes, Bobby Jones was engulfed by thousands of people who had heard he was on the golf course, and they watched him finish right there at the 18th hole. And when I was going up there, I had an inkling of what Bobby Jones probably felt."

What I have felt since first encountering Watson was how much he valued integrity, both in the rules and within the spirit of the game. When he was a freshman at Stanford University, the winter of 1968, he qualified for match play in the San Francisco City Golf Championship at Harding Park.

Watson had hit into a row of eucalyptus trees to the right side of the par-5 10th. When he hit out, the small gallery and his opponent believed it was his second shot. Watson, however, pointed out that, unseen by any except himself, he had moved the ball a fraction of an inch and was lying 3. He would lose the hole, but win respect.

It was Jones, of course, who insisted after being praised for calling a stroke on himself for inadvertently striking the ball in the 1925 US Open: "You might as well praise a man for not robbing a bank. There is only one way to play the game."

Tom Watson always played it elegantly and most times splendidly. He didn't at first like the peculiarities of links golf, the unfair bounces, the difficult conditions. Eventually he understood the beauty of a sport that could be as frustrating as it was rewarding.

Watson had so many Open moments, especially beating Jack Nicklaus in 1977 at Turnberry, the Duel in the Sun, two of the best playing their best. Then 32 years later, at the same course, Watson, 59, somehow went into the 72nd hole with the lead before an approach rolled off the green and reality rolled in. Stewart Cink would win the play-off, and Watson would advise a press corps disappointed in his failure to create history, "This ain't no funeral."

Neither was his farewell at St Andrews. On the contrary, for Tom Watson and all who have felt his presence through the decades, the 2015 Open Championship was a good walk down Memory Lane, a mythical path that begins where the 18th fairway of the Old Course ends.

*Brian Harman, USA*

*David Hearn, Canada*

*Andy Sullivan, England*

*Søren Kjeldsen, Denmark*

**144**[TH]
**ST ANDREWS**

## AMERICA

| | |
|---|---|
| Travelers Championship | 25-28 June |
| **Brian Harman, USA** | |
| **Graham DeLaet, Canada** | |
| **Carl Pettersson, Sweden** | |
| **Luke Donald, England** | |
| Greenbrier Classic | 2-5 July |
| **David Hearn, Canada** | |
| **Danny Lee, New Zealand** | |
| **James Hahn, USA** | |
| **Greg Owen, England** | |
| John Deere Classic | 9-12 July |
| **Tom Gillis, USA** | |

THE
**OPEN**
QUALIFYING SERIES

## AFRICA

| | |
|---|---|
| Joberg Open | 26 Feb - 1 Mar |
| **Andy Sullivan, England** | |
| **Anthony Wall, England** | |
| **David Howell, England** | |

*Raphaël Jacquelin, France*

*Taichi Teshima, Japan*

*Marcus Fraser, Australia*

*Rod Pampling, Australia*

## EUROPE

**Dubai Duty Free Irish Open**     28-31 May
**Søren Kjeldsen, Denmark**
**Eddie Pepperell, England**
**Tyrrell Hatton, England**

**Alstom Open de France**     2-5 July
**James Morrison, England**
**Jaco Van Zyl, South Africa**
**Rafa Cabrera-Bello, Spain**

**Aberdeen Asset Management**
**Scottish Open**     9-12 July
**Raphaël Jacquelin, France**
**Daniel Brooks, England**
**Rikard Karlberg, Sweden**

### FINAL QUALIFYING

**Gailes Links**     30 June
**Mark Young, England**
**Paul Kinnear*(P), England**
**Ryan Fox(P), New Zealand**

**Hillside**     30 June
**Scott Arnold, Australia**
**Jordan Niebrugge*, USA**
**Pelle Edberg, Sweden**

**Royal Cinque Ports**     30 June
**Alister Balcombe*, England**
**Benjamin Taylor*, England**
**Gary Boyd, England**

**Woburn**     30 June
**Paul Dunne*, Republic of Ireland**
**Robert Dinwiddie, England**
**Retief Goosen(P), South Africa**

*Denotes amateur     (P)Qualified after play-off

## JAPAN

**Mizuno Open**     28-31 May
**Taichi Teshima, Japan**
**Scott Strange, Australia**
**Tadahiro Takayama, Japan**
**Shinji Tomimura, Japan**

## THAILAND

**Thailand Golf Championship**     11-14 Dec
**Marcus Fraser, Australia**
**Scott Hend, Australia**
**Jonathan Moore, USA**
**Anirban Lahiri, India**

## AUSTRALIA

**Emirates Australian Open**     27-30 Nov
**Rod Pampling, Australia**
**Brett Rumford, Australia**
**Greg Chalmers, Australia**

# EXEMPT COMPETITORS

*Tom Watson*

*Sir Nick Faldo*

*Jason Day*

*Padraig Harrington*

| Name, Country | Category |
|---|---|
| Thomas Aiken, South Africa | 18 |
| Byeong-Hun An, Korea | 7 |
| Kiradech Aphibarnrat, Thailand | 8 |
| Daniel Berger, USA | 5 |
| Thomas Bjørn, Denmark | 6,15 |
| Adam Bland, Australia | 21 |
| Jonas Blixt, Sweden | 6 |
| Steven Bowditch, Australia | 14 |
| Keegan Bradley, USA | 5,11,15 |
| Mark Calcavecchia, USA | 1,3 |
| Paul Casey, England | 5 |
| Greg Chalmers, Australia | 17 |
| Ashley Chesters*, England | 25 |
| Stewart Cink, USA | 1,2,3 |
| Darren Clarke, Northern Ireland | 1,2,3 |
| George Coetzee, South Africa | 6 |
| Ben Curtis, USA | 1 |
| John Daly, USA | 1 |
| Jason Day, Australia | 5,13 |
| Jamie Donaldson, Wales | 5,6,15 |
| Victor Dubuisson, France | 4,5,6,15 |
| Jason Dufner, USA | 11 |
| David Duval, USA | 1 |
| Ernie Els, South Africa | 1,2,3 |
| Harris English, USA | 5 |
| Matt Every, USA | 5 |
| Sir Nick Faldo, England | 1 |
| Ross Fisher, England | 6 |
| Tommy Fleetwood, England | 6 |
| Rickie Fowler, USA | 4,5,12,13,15 |
| Hiroyuki Fujita, Japan | 20 |
| Jim Furyk, USA | 4,5,13,15 |
| Stephen Gallacher, Scotland | 6,15 |
| Sergio Garcia, Spain | 4,5,6,13,15 |
| Branden Grace, South Africa | 5 |
| Bill Haas, USA | 5,13 |
| Todd Hamilton, USA | 1 |
| Padraig Harrington, Republic of Ireland | 1,2 |
| Russell Henley, USA | 13 |
| Charley Hoffman, USA | 14 |
| Morgan Hoffmann, USA | 13 |
| JB Holmes, USA | 5 |
| Billy Horschel, USA | 5,13 |
| Yuta Ikeda, Japan | 19 |
| Mikko Ilonen, Finland | 6 |
| Hiroshi Iwata**, Japan | 5 |
| Thongchai Jaidee, Thailand | 5,6 |
| Miguel Angel Jiménez, Spain | 5,6 |
| Dustin Johnson, USA | 5,13 |
| Zach Johnson, USA | 5,13,15 |
| Matt Jones, Australia | 5 |
| Martin Kaymer, Germany | 5,6,9,11,12,13,15 |
| Kevin Kisner, USA | 14 |
| Russell Knox**, Scotland | 5 |
| Brooks Koepka, USA | 5,6 |
| Matt Kuchar, USA | 5,13,15 |
| Anirban Lahiri, India | 5 |
| Romain Langasque*, France | 23 |

| Name, Country | Category |
|---|---|
| Bernhard Langer, Germany | 22 |
| Pablo Larrazábal, Spain | 6 |
| Paul Lawrie, Scotland | 1 |
| Tom Lehman, USA | 1 |
| Marc Leishman, Australia | 4 |
| Justin Leonard, USA | 1,3 |
| Alexander Levy, France | 6 |
| Liang Wen-chong, China | 21 |
| David Lingmerth, Sweden | 5 |
| David Lipsky, USA | 16 |
| Shane Lowry, Republic of Ireland | 4,5,6 |
| Joost Luiten, Netherlands | 5,6 |
| Sandy Lyle, Scotland | 1 |
| Hunter Mahan, USA | 5,13,15 |
| Matteo Manassero, Italy | 7 |
| Ben Martin, USA | 5 |
| Hideki Matsuyama, Japan | 5,13 |
| Graeme McDowell, N. Ireland | 4,5,6,15 |
| Phil Mickelson, USA | 1,2,3,5,15 |
| Edoardo Molinari, Italy | 4 |
| Francesco Molinari, Italy | 5 |
| Ryan Moore, USA | 5 |
| Kevin Na, USA | 5,13 |
| Koumei Oda, Japan | 20 |
| Geoff Ogilvy, Australia | 13 |
| Mark O'Meara, USA | 1 |
| Louis Oosthuizen, South Africa | 1,2,3,5,6 |
| Ryan Palmer, USA | 5,13 |
| Ian Poulter, England | 5,6,15 |
| Richie Ramsay**, Scotland | 5 |
| Patrick Reed, USA | 5,13,15 |
| Justin Rose, England | 5,6,9,13,15 |
| Oliver Schniederjans*, USA | 26 |
| Charl Schwartzel, South Africa | 4,5,6,10 |
| Adam Scott, Australia | 4,5,10,13 |
| John Senden, Australia | 13 |
| Marcel Siem, Germany | 6 |
| Webb Simpson, USA | 5,9,13,15 |
| Brandt Snedeker, USA | 5 |
| Jordan Spieth, USA | 5,9,10,13,15 |
| Henrik Stenson, Sweden | 5,6,15 |
| Robert Streb, USA | 14 |
| Kevin Streelman**, USA | 5 |
| Brendon Todd, USA | 5,13 |
| Cameron Tringale, USA | 13 |
| Jimmy Walker, USA | 5,13,15 |
| Marc Warren, Scotland | 6 |
| Bubba Watson, USA | 5,10,13,15 |
| Tom Watson, USA | 3 |
| Romain Wattel, France | 6 |
| Lee Westwood, England | 5,6,15 |
| Bernd Wiesberger, Austria | 5 |
| Danny Willett, England | 5,6 |
| Gary Woodland, USA | 5,13 |
| Tiger Woods, USA | 1,2,3,12 |
| Gunn Yang*, Korea | 24 |

*Denotes amateur     **Denotes reserve

*Jordan Spieth*

*Paul Lawrie*

*Tiger Woods*

*Louis Oosthuizen*

# KEY TO EXEMPTIONS FROM THE OPEN QUALIFYING SERIES

Exemptions for 2015 were granted to the following:

(1)  The Open Champions aged 60 or under on 19 July 2015.

(2)  The Open Champions for 2005-2014.

(3)  The Open Champions finishing in the first 10 and tying for 10th place in The Open Championship 2009-2014.

(4)  First 10 and anyone tying for 10th place in the 2014 Open Championship at Royal Liverpool.

(5)  The first 50 players on the Official World Golf Ranking for Week 21, 2015.

(6)  First 30 in the Race to Dubai for 2014.

(7)  The BMW PGA Championship winners for 2013-2015.

(8)  First 5 European Tour members and any European Tour members tying for 5th place, not otherwise exempt, in the top 20 of the Race to Dubai on completion of the 2015 BMW International Open.

(9)  The US Open Champions for 2011-2015.

(10)  The Masters Tournament Champions for 2011-2015.

(11)  The PGA Champions for 2010-2014.

(12)  The PLAYERS Champions for 2013-2015.

(13)  The leading 30 qualifiers for the 2014 TOUR CHAMPI-ONSHIP.

(14)  First 5 PGA TOUR members and any PGA TOUR members tying for 5th place, not exempt in the top 20 of the PGA TOUR FedExCup Points List for 2015 on completion of the 2015 Travelers Championship.

(15)  Playing members of the 2014 Ryder Cup Teams.

(16)  First and anyone tying for 1st place on the Order of Merit of the Asian Tour for 2014.

(17)  First and anyone tying for 1st place on the Order of Merit of the Tour of Australasia for 2014.

(18)  First and anyone tying for 1st place on the Order of Merit of the Southern Africa PGA Sunshine Tour for 2014.

(19)  The Japan Open Champion for 2014.

(20)  First 2 and anyone tying for 2nd place, on the Official Money List of the Japan Golf Tour for 2014.

(21)  First 2 and anyone tying for 2nd place, not exempt having applied OQS Japan, in a cumulative money list taken from all official 2015 Japan Golf Tour events up to and including the 2015 Japan Tour Championship.

(22)  The Senior Open Champion for 2014.

(23)  The Amateur Champion for 2015.

(24)  The US Amateur Champion for 2014.

(25)  The International European Amateur Champion for 2014.

(26)  The Mark H McCormack Medal (Men's World Amateur Golf Ranking™) winner for 2014.

# Golf's Homecoming

*By Andy Farrell*

Opens at St Andrews always provide the game with a special homecoming. It is here, where golf began, that the past is honoured even as its history grows deeper. So it was in 2015.

Around every corner of the Old Course can be found tales to be told and traditions to be respected. A trip to the Home of Golf is a sacred pilgrimage for any golfer. "For those that love the game, this needs to be on their bucket list," said Zach Johnson, the new Champion Golfer of the Year. But to play for the Claret Jug that Johnson now holds, golf's greatest prize, on these ancient links is the greatest privilege of all. For newcomer and returning veteran alike.

It applied to Alister Balcombe, a 19-year-old amateur, who had never even stepped foot in the place before he made it through two stages of qualifying inspired by seeing a big picture of the scene at the 18th hole in a magazine and thinking: "Wouldn't

*Holes 1, 17 & 18: a historic arena with seating for 10,000.*

it be great to be a part of that!" — as well as to five-time Champion Tom Watson, who came to say farewell and managed it without the tears that flowed when he accompanied Jack Nicklaus' last walk in 2005.

Sir Nick Faldo also waved goodbye, from the Swilcan Bridge where, in 1990, he scratched his studs on the ancient stonework because, he said, "I wanted to leave my mark next to the scuffs of all the other past St Andrews Champions." Louis Oosthuizen, so close to repeating as a St Andrews Champion, felt a tingle as he finished his first practice round on Monday. He was playing with Branden Grace, whose caddie Zach Rasego was alongside Oosthuizen five years earlier. "The two of us looked at each other and smiled," Oosthuizen said. "It was great to do that walk again, remembering that moment from 2010, and feel that bit of magic around here."

There have now been 29 Championships played on the Old Course and links with the past abound. A flooded course? Try 1873, the very first Open at St Andrews, when the winner, Tom Kidd, was the first to receive the Claret Jug. He just managed to resist the temptation to sell it, but the £11 first prize enabled the penniless caddie to get engaged

# ST ANDREWS CHAMPIONS

Zach Johnson became the 24th player to claim the Claret Jug in the 29 Opens played at St Andrews, while Louis Oosthuizen just missed out on being the fifth player to win successive titles on the Old Course:

| | |
|---|---|
| 1873 | Tom Kidd |
| 1876 | Bob Martin |
| 1879 | Jamie Anderson |
| 1882 | Bob Ferguson |
| 1885 | Bob Martin |
| 1888 | Jack Burns |
| 1891 | Hugh Kirkaldy |
| 1895 | JH Taylor |
| 1900 | JH Taylor |
| 1905 | James Braid |
| 1910 | James Braid |
| 1921 | Jock Hutchison |
| 1927 | Bobby Jones* |
| 1933 | Denny Shute |
| 1939 | Dick Burton |
| 1946 | Sam Snead |
| 1955 | Peter Thomson |
| 1957 | Bobby Locke |
| 1960 | Kel Nagle |
| 1964 | Tony Lema |
| 1970 | Jack Nicklaus |
| 1978 | Jack Nicklaus |
| 1984 | Seve Ballesteros |
| 1990 | Nick Faldo |
| 1995 | John Daly |
| 2000 | Tiger Woods |
| 2005 | Tiger Woods |
| 2010 | Louis Oosthuizen |
| 2015 | Zach Johnson |

*Denotes amateur

*The Old Course was presented in immaculate condition thanks to the efforts of*

to his beloved Eliza and he did sell the Gold Medal to pay for the wedding. How times have changed!

There was another flooding in 1960, at the Centenary Open, which also went into an extra day. Arnold Palmer, winner of the Masters and the US Open that year, came up one stroke short of the brave Australian Kel Nagle, who died early in 2015. How spookily similar was the ending to Jordan Spieth's own quest for a Grand Slam?

More than anyone, the name of Bobby Jones leapt out of the past and into the present conversation. The last amateur to lead after 54 holes (1927). The last amateur Champion (1930). The only player to achieve a calendar-year Grand Slam (also 1930). Watson referenced the time Jones returned for a friendly game on the Old Course and the townsfolk spilled onto the links to welcome back "Our Bobby."

Then there was the emotional ceremony at Younger Hall in 1958 when Jones received the freedom of the city and said: "I could take out of my life everything except my experiences at St Andrews and I'd still have had a full rich life." That grand university hall saw another great ceremony at the start of the week in 2015 when 1998 Champion Mark O'Meara and Britain's greatest female golfer, Laura Davies, were among those inducted into the World Golf Hall of Fame.

But it was Johnson's victory that made the most pertinent link with Jones, and the course and the tournament he founded: Augusta National and the Masters. Johnson became the 14th player to win both the Masters Tournament and The Open and the sixth to triumph at both Augusta and St Andrews. In fact, seven of the last nine Opens at St

*the greenkeeping staff of St Andrews Links Trust, who worked tirelessly especially in the extreme weather later in the week.*

Andrews have been won by Masters Champions. Of the other two, Oosthuizen lost a play-off at Augusta in 2012 and John Daly finished third there in 1993.

This is a remarkable correlation but hardly surprising given that Jones and his co-designer at Augusta, Alister MacKenzie, were both "extravagant admirers" of the Old Course. MacKenzie prized a hole like the 11th, where "under certain conditions it is extremely difficult for even the best player that ever breathed, especially if he is attempting to get a 2, but at the same time an inferior player may get a 4 if he plays his own game exceptionally well."

Jones detested American courses that could only be played one way and came to love the opportunity varying conditions on a British links gave a golfer to test their strategic talent. "There is always some little favour of wind or terrain waiting for the man who has judgment enough to use it, and there is a little feeling of triumph, a thrill that comes with the knowledge of having done a thing well when a puzzling hole has been conquered by something more than mechanical skill."

The pair combined their ideals into Augusta National, and Leonard Crawley, the Walker Cup player and *Daily Telegraph* correspondent, could

*Earlier in the year The Open lost its then oldest Champion.*

see the St Andrews influence when he played there in 1947. "They have not copied one single hole on those maddeningly difficult and infinitely fascinating links," he wrote, "but they have built 18 great holes, every one of which is perfectly fair and demands that a player first and foremost use his brains."

St Andrews is not always fair but remains just as much a puzzle to solve as Augusta. Jones, who admitted he fell in love with the Old Course the more he studied it, certainly found it maddening on his first visit. After taking too many blows to escape Hill bunker on the 11th in 1921 he tore up his card. He returned in triumph at the 1927 Open and the 1930 Amateur Championship.

Many others have had to revise their first impres-

*Younger Hall was the scene of the World Golf Hall of Fame Induction Ceremony that included 1998 Champion Mark O'Meara.*

sions, including Watson, who hated the place in 1978 despite already having won two Opens by then. Sam Snead spied an "abandoned golf course" from the train as he arrived in St Andrews for the first time in 1946, only to master the links and become Open Champion. It is the railways that have abandoned the town, while golf continues to thrive.

Henry Longhurst wrote of his first round on the Old Course: "It put me in mind of the early stages of a jigsaw puzzle, when all one has done is a few bits of sky. It was not until I had played half a dozen rounds on it that I began to catch the magic. After 20 rounds or so I began to know something about it, and to perceive the almost limitless extent of what remained yet to be found out."

"The reason the course is so interesting the more you play it is because it's a course with infinite shades of grey," said Australian Geoff Ogilvy, who admitted it is the only course in the world where he throws away the yardage book and relies on feel for whether a particular bunker is in play given the conditions.

Faldo, who arrived this year armed with caddie Fanny Sunesson's yardage book from 1990, was helped to victory by notes given to him by Gerald Micklem, a former Captain of the Royal and Ancient Golf Club, listing specific targets on each hole for differing weather conditions. "You've got to plot the shots, you've got to understand the wind direction, where you're going to land it, where it's going to release, all the downslopes, all the upslopes," Faldo explained. "You've got to take everything in."

Faldo found only one bunker throughout the 1990 Open, which seemed amazing until Tiger Woods missed the lot 10 years later. Mind you, Rickie Fowler repeated that feat in 2010, only to find a whole heap of other trouble in an opening 79.

Prior to a Championship which started with one Johnson (Dustin) overpowering the course and ended with another Johnson (Zach) tacking his way to victory, Woods had said: "The first thing I ever heard about St Andrews is that all you do is hit it as hard as you can and aim left. That's basically not how you play the course. You need to have the

*"The Loop" out by the Eden Estuary gives the Old Course its shepherd's crook shape.*

right angles. A five-degree wind change here changes the whole golf course completely. I've always found that fascinating."

About the only thing overpowering the links in 2015 was the gale on Saturday, when play was suspended. This despite the softening of the slope on the 11th green to bring Jones' Hill bunker back into play, which was among the changes made since the last Open. Others included the first bunker changes for half a century.

For some, any change to the Old Course is controversial, but the constant evolution of the game at St Andrews means it is informed by the past, not locked into it. Where to draw the line — back when there were 22 holes, only single fairways and greens played in both directions, when the course played left-handed rather than right-handed as today? Woods, for one, might plump for the last since he revealed that "before I die I want to play it one time backwards. That would be a blast."

On the eve of his last Open as Chief Executive of The R&A, Peter Dawson was asked if it was conceivable that the Old Course might in the future be inadequate to challenge professional golfers. "No, it has stood the test of time," he replied. "The players love playing it. They don't feel under-challenged by it. There are so many subtleties of ground and wind out there that the Old Course will last well into the future as a strong challenge."

66 *St Andrews is one of those places where you can be the only person around but you feel like people are watching you. It's got that aura about it. The hairs on the back of your neck stand up.* 99
—*Justin Rose*

66 *For everything that is said about the course at St Andrews, maybe not enough is said about the people. LOVE their golf.* 99
—*Webb Simpson*

# Thomson and The King star again

*Peter Dixon enjoys a memorable celebration at the Champion Golfers' Challenge.*

*Peter Thomson won over the Old Course 60 years ago.*

Could there have been a more fitting way to get the 144TH Open up and running than with the Champion Golfers' Challenge on the eve of the Championship?

Spectators gathered in their thousands to pay tribute to some of the game's finest players, who between them boasted 44 Open and 83 Major victories spanning a period of 60 years. Part of a pretty exclusive club, the 28 former Champions were divided into seven teams of four and played four holes in total — the first, second, 17th and 18th.

Appropriately, each of the Champions was announced onto the first tee by Ivor Robson, in his 41st and final year as official starter, and how they all rose to the occasion — from Louis Oosthuizen, the youngest at 32, to Peter Thomson, the oldest at 86. Needless to say, there was plenty to watch and to admire.

One of the loudest cheers was reserved for Arnold Palmer, 85, who has been such a champion of The Open over the years and who had obviously lost none

of the charisma for which he became renowned. After hitting a "ceremonial" tee-shot off the first — "Only my second swing this year," he informed the galleries — The King, as he is affectionately known, chose to hit only one more shot before walking the rest of the way in the company of his team-mates, Paul Lawrie, Darren Clarke and Bill Rogers.

And such was the support he received from start to finish that he was left almost speechless. In response he would raise his arms and give a gentle bow. "I looked at these stands and they were full of people. It was amazing," he said. "I feel very honoured to have been given such a reception."

What better place than St Andrews and the Old Course to celebrate the careers of such players, among them Tony Jacklin, Ernie Els and Sandy Lyle? There was mutual respect, a sharing of anecdotes as they walked the hallowed fairways and, for the likes of Oosthuizen and Padraig Harrington, a whetting of the appetite.

"That really gets the juices flowing," said Harrington, Champion in 2007 and 2008. "It was great to be a part of it, to be called to the tee as a former Champion. It's nice to be with fellow Champions and legends of the game and to realise you are forever linked with them. It reminds you of what you've achieved and makes you want to do it again."

Among the shots of the day was one from "local hero" Lawrie, who found the hole from out of rough

*Gary Player's swing showed he was as fit as ever.*

*Arnold Palmer led his team to victory (right).*

at the par-4 second for a superb eagle. He then added a birdie for good measure at the 18th that drew his side level with three others on three under par but brought victory courtesy of his team having the highest average age. Now that's what you call a countback!

"I haven't played with Arnold before, so it was a dream come true," said Lawrie, winner at Carnoustie in 1999.

Everywhere you looked there were glimpses of the past. At 79, New Zealand's Sir Bob Charles, the first left-hander to win a Major, looked every bit as elegant standing over the ball as he did in his heyday. And if ever a player looked as if he might be ready to go another 72 holes, it was Gary Player, fit as a butcher's dog at 79, who milked the applause after almost finding the hole with his approach shot to the second.

While Phil Mickelson, Champion at Muirfield in 2013, may have had his eyes on the week's main prize, he nonetheless revelled in playing alongside Thomson, who won the second of five Claret Jugs at St Andrews in 1955. "This event was helping to celebrate Peter's victory 60 years ago — and to be part of that made me very proud," Mickelson said.

Among other moments, Sir Nick Faldo donned the jumper he had worn on his way to victory in 1990; Tiger Woods birdied the fearsome 17th; and every single player posed for photographs on the Swilcan Bridge. It was a perfect end to a perfect start.

*Tiger Woods*

*Louis Oosthuizen and Ian Baker-Finch*

# Dustin Powers Into the Lead

*By Andy Farrell*

Two Saturdays prior to the 144TH Open two things happened that would have a significant impact on the Championship. Given the date, 4 July, would the omens be good for the American challenge at St Andrews?

That morning there was such a deluge at the Home of Golf that any chance of the Old Course playing dry, firm and fast became unrealistic. Regular downpours subsequently ensured a soft, green links. Think Hoylake 2014 rather than Muirfield 2013.

Think Hoylake, think Rory McIlroy. But the same day at home in Northern Ireland, McIlroy ruptured an ankle ligament in a kickabout game of football with friends. There would be no world No 1 at St Andrews and, for the first time since 1954, no defending Champion. The Claret Jug was returned, but McIlroy did not get the chance to win it back on a course that he adores and where he scored a 63 in the opening round in 2010.

*Dustin Johnson went out in 31 during his seven-under-par 65.*

He was missed, how could he not be? But one look at the leaderboard after the first round confirmed that any number of world class players would be in contention for the title. In fact, it was almost as if the game's elite had continued on from the US Open the previous month.

There was Jordan Spieth, winner of the first two Majors of the year, on 67, alongside one of the runners-up from Chambers Bay, Louis Oosthuizen, the 2010 Open Champion. And the other runner-up, Dustin Johnson, was leading the way on 65. Jason Day, another of the stirring stories from Seattle after his battle with vertigo, was among those on 66. "That's amazing, isn't it?" Day said. "Bloody hell, they just won't go away. It's good excitement for the game. It's kind of extended on from the US Open with Dustin Johnson and Jordan Spieth where they are right now, so it's going to be an exciting three days coming up."

It was already a crowded leaderboard, with Johnson out on his own at seven under par, one ahead of Day, local favourite Paul Lawrie, England's Danny Willett, double US Open Champion Retief Goosen, and Americans Robert Streb and Zach Johnson, no relation. With Spieth and Oosthuizen on five

*Australia's Rod Pampling had the honour of teeing off first at 6.32am in front of the Royal and Ancient Clubhouse.*

*US Open revisited: Jordan Spieth and Dustin Johnson.*

under par were the latter's fellow South African Charl Schwartzel, Kevin Na and American amateur Jordan Niebrugge.

Dustin Johnson had also led after the first round of the US Open, but it is what happened at the end that was still fresh in the memory. While Spieth birdied the 72nd hole, Johnson saw his downhill, eagle-putt for victory run past the hole and he ended up missing the one back.

This was Johnson's first outing since and, having climbed to the top of the leaderboard, he was immediately fending off media enquiries about how he had put his disappointment behind him. He is not a man to dwell on the past. "Well, you know,

*After winning the Masters and the US Open, Jordan Spieth received a warm welcome at St Andrews.*

nothing bad happened at Chambers Bay," he quietly insisted. "I was disappointed, really. I played well, I did everything I was supposed to do. I couldn't control what the ball was doing on the greens there. There really are no bad feelings from that, only good. I played really well and that carried over to today."

What made his performance all the more impressive was that he was drawn for the first two rounds with Japan's Hideki Matsuyama and the man he lost to at Chambers Bay, Spieth. To Johnson they were just two "buddies who like playing with each other."

Spieth said: "It was an unfortunate ending to the US Open, but today we just got off to a normal round of golf like always and were actually able to feed off each other and enjoy the day. It's not like he really messed up at Chambers. I think he played extremely well and I expected him to continue playing well because he really doesn't play bad ever. I expect him to be a guy to beat every single time you play. He's got as much talent, or more, than anybody."

Johnson got to display that talent on a morning that started calmly, before the wind got up as the day went on, and with the first nine playing on average three strokes easier than the inward half. Sweden's David Lingmerth went to the turn in 29, equalling the St Andrews Open record, with eight 3s and a par-5 at the fifth. Johnson's outward 31 could not have been more simply compiled. Wedge approaches produced birdies at the second and third, while a driver and a 7-iron

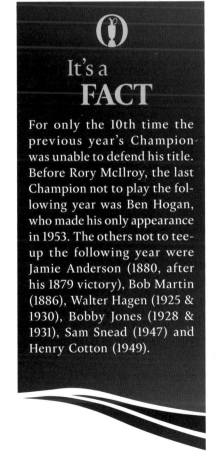

**It's a FACT**

For only the 10th time the previous year's Champion was unable to defend his title. Before Rory McIlroy, the last Champion not to play the following year was Ben Hogan, who made his only appearance in 1953. The others not to tee-up the following year were Jamie Anderson (1880, after his 1879 victory), Bob Martin (1886), Walter Hagen (1925 & 1930), Bobby Jones (1928 & 1931), Sam Snead (1947) and Henry Cotton (1949).

"The juxtaposition of Johnson's power off the tee and Spieth's precision into the greens was worth donning ski caps and parkas and venturing out into a cold summer's day."

—**Karen Crouse,**
*New York Times*

"Faldo, the game's greatest Englishman, knew the risk he was taking stepping out of the TV commentary box in the United States to immerse himself once more in the mystique of St Andrews."

—**Kevin Garside,**
*The Independent*

"As a gauge of Johnson's excellence, he is the first player since Gary Player in 1974 to hold the first round lead at both the US Open and Open."

—**James Corrigan,**
*Daily Telegraph*

"Jordan Spieth played like he had a Grand Slam to win. Dustin Johnson played like he had a score to settle. The two main characters from Chambers Bay brought their games across eight time zones and an ocean and set the tone at St Andrews for what could be another riveting battle at The Open."

—**Doug Ferguson,**
*Press Association*

*Louis Oosthuizen and Jason Day react as Louis' putt just misses at the fifth.*

to 10 feet led to an eagle at the fifth. At the ninth, he drove the front of the green and two-putted for a 3.

Since missing the cut on his debut in 2009, Johnson had only once fared worse than the 14th place he recorded at St Andrews in 2010. The runner-up in 2011 at Royal St George's, he has put together a strong record on links golf. "And this is one of my favourite Open venues, but then it's hard to beat St Andrews for an Open Championship," he said. "It sets up well for me. I think it challenges every part of your game."

Johnson also birdied the 10th after a short pitch to six feet but then displayed his quality with the long clubs that fills even his fellow competitors with awe. At the inward par 5, the 14th, he hit a driver and a 3-wood from 275 yards to six feet, almost pin high

*Tiger Woods got off to an unfortunate start by finding the Swilcan Burn with his second shot at the first hole.*

(and missed the putt for his second eagle of the day). Paul Casey had watched on television and could not help musing on the difference in the afternoon when the wind against had strengthened considerably. "I hit driver, 3-iron, 5-iron," he said. "Dustin is a lot longer than I am, but still, that's a massive difference."

At the 16th, Johnson was just short with a 6-iron from 200 yards and at the 17th he was again short, this time with a 4-iron from 220 yards. "They were the only times I was out of position and I made a 10-footer and a 15-footer for pars," he said. "Other than that I had looks at birdie all day."

*Kevin Na was among those on five-under-par 67.*

*Danny Willett enjoyed his birdie at the last.*

There was not a dropped stroke on his card and it was Spieth who summed up the ease of the leader's round. "If DJ keeps driving it the way he is, then I'm going to have to play my best golf to have a chance," he said. "It's hard to argue with somebody who's splitting bunkers at about 380 yards and just two-putting for birdie on five or six holes when there's only two par 5s. I don't have that in my bag, so I've got to make up for it with ball-striking."

Not that Spieth was raising the white flag. "I've played enough golf with him to believe in my skill-set and that I can still trump that crazy ability he has," Spieth said in the understated but emphatic tone that we have come to know. "I expect when he stands on the tee it's going to be up there miles down the fairway. I also expect that I can birdie each hole when I stand on the tee. It just happens to be a little different route."

## Lingmerth makes his mark with record equalling 29

When David Lingmerth reached the turn in the first round of The Open in just 29 strokes, he may have been forgiven for thinking he had unlocked the secret to playing the Old Course. The 27-year-old US-based Swede, making his debut in the Championship, equalled the record for the front nine in an Open at St Andrews, a score shared by just three others — Tony Jacklin (1970), Ian Baker-Finch and Paul Broadhurst (both 1990).

The scoring stretched credulity. After opening his round with four birdies in succession, the Memorial Tournament winner added three more, at the sixth, seventh and ninth, with his only pars coming at the par-5 fifth and the par-3 eighth. His 29 was made up of eight 3s and a solitary 5.

Most tantalising was the prospect of the first sub-63 round in the history of Major Championships. If only it were that easy. The Old Lady does not give up her records that readily, however, and having first seduced the Swede, she then stung him. His inward nine? A demoralising 40 that included three bogeys and a double-bogey at the Road Hole.

"I did not know about the record," Lingmerth said. "It's a pretty special feeling. I was obviously feeling really good and trying not to think too much. I felt good on the back nine, too, just in links golf you can miss 30 yards one way and be fine, and if you miss three feet the wrong way, you're in big trouble.

"I'm definitely learning as I go, and I definitely learned the hard way on the back today."

—Peter Dixon

*Phil Mickelson's Open got off course when he tangled with the bushes on the sixth.*

With McIlroy not around, Spieth's quest for the Grand Slam was the focus of attention. It was a shame, however, not to have a showdown between the two to rival that of 43 years earlier. Jack Nicklaus won the first two Majors of 1972, after Lee Trevino had won the last two of 1971. At Muirfield, Trevino beat Nicklaus by one stroke.

With such small margins at stake, and history on the line, the decision of the Masters and US Open Champion to honour his commitment to the John Deere Classic, instead of opting for extra practice on the Old Course, where he had played only once before in a friendly game prior to the 2011 Walker Cup, came under intense scrutiny. Instead, he set up the Old Course on his golf simulator at his home in Texas.

"It was fun and it didn't hurt to see some of the lines, but I'm in no way saying that's what I did to prepare for this Open," he said. "Everything changes

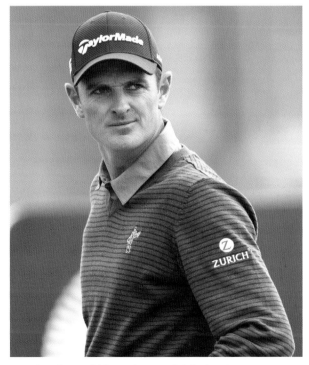

*Despite a late wobble Justin Rose finished on 71.*

*Japan's Hiroyuki Fujita chips from beside the road behind the 17th green. He made his par.*

*John Daly and caddie Anna Cladakis*

here depending on the wind, so the real preparation started when we got over here."

Spieth arrived having won the John Deere event, as he had in 2013, and his form appeared to have travelled nicely as he opened with two birdies before adding three in a row from the fifth. He matched Johnson's outward 31, then had a 2 at the 11th before a slightly stuttering finish. He dropped shots at the 13th and the 17th, but got down in a pitch and a putt for a 3 at the last, something he would have offered much gold for four days later.

Despite all that he had achieved so far in his career, at 21 Spieth was actually younger than many of the nine amateurs in the field. From the off they showed they would be a force during the week. Ireland's Paul Dunne holed a huge putt on the ninth to get to four under par before signing for a 69.

Niebrugge posted a 67 — to tie Joe Carr's record for an amateur at St Andrews — thanks in part to an acclimatisation that included playing in The Amateur Championship at Carnoustie and the Bra-

*Jason Day got into contention with an opening 66.*

# Day healthy again; his idol Tiger ailing

Last seen, Jason Day was collapsing with vertigo at the US Open and yet still managing to finish in the top 10 at Chambers Bay. An opening 66 at St Andrews put his health in the spotlight again, but with better news. "I feel healthy and I'm good to go," said the 27-year-old Australian. "I'm not thinking about falling over on my face again."

Day first suffered from the symptoms in 2010 and after consulting his doctors again felt confident about managing the condition. "Being on the medicine I'm on right now definitely helps," he said. "I know if I have it, it takes a couple of days to get rid of. Obviously it's not great to have it in a tournament but I can't control that."

Day was playing with the two most recent St Andrews Champions in Louis Oosthuizen, who was also in contention with a 67, and Tiger Woods, who was not, after a 76. Woods never got going after finding the Swilcan Burn with his approach shot at the first hole. He started with two bogeys and went out in 40 despite the calm morning conditions.

It was hard to watch for Day, who followed his career as a youngster and is now friends with the former world No 1. "He was my idol growing up. He's why I chased the dream of being a professional. It's unfortunate to see him like this. It's just tough to see your idol struggle."

—*Andy Farrell*

*By round's end the figures on Tiger's card added up to a 76.*

*Luke Donald played a miraculous shot from under the lip of the Road Hole Bunker...*

*Jordan Niebrugge led the amateurs on 67.*

*Ireland's Paul Dunne went out in 32 on the way to a 69.*

*...while Marc Warren almost holed his recovery from the historic hazard.*

bazon Trophy before trying his luck in Final Qualifying at Hillside. Amateur Champion Romain Langasque joined Dunne on 69, while American Oliver Schniederjans had a 70. Late in the day Ashley Chesters, twice the European Amateur Champion, began a rollercoaster week by racing to five under par after an eagle at the 10th, only to drop four strokes in the last three holes.

Easily done. Lee Westwood bogeyed the last three and Justin Rose three of the last six for 71 apiece. Rose had to remind himself that it was an event played over 72 holes, and not 18. "Otherwise you'd hang up your boots at the 17th and have a pint in the Jigger Inn," he sighed. He was playing with Britain's greatest modern golfer in Sir Nick Faldo, but the 1990 Champion at St Andrews needed stronger sustenance after propping up the field with an 83, seven more than 65-year-old Tom Watson.

Luke Donald played a miraculous shot from under the lip of the Road Hole Bunker, revealing that he had had extra practice from sand as a "replica" bunker had been sunk into the garden of the house he was staying in. Living up to its fearsome reputation, the 17th did not yield a single birdie all day. Marc Warren almost holed out from the old beast as he matched Donald's 68, but Lawrie took

*Oliver Schniederjans and his fans.*

*Dustin Johnson shows off his athletic talent with another huge drive at the 13th hole.*

*Spieth offers his congratulations.*

## Round of the Day: Dustin Johnson – 65

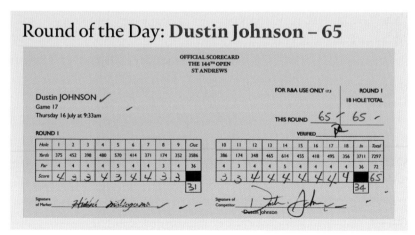

OFFICIAL SCORECARD
THE 144TH OPEN
ST ANDREWS

Dustin JOHNSON ✓
Game 17
Thursday 16 July at 9:33am

FOR R&A USE ONLY (7.3)    ROUND 1
18 HOLE TOTAL

THIS ROUND  65   65

VERIFIED

ROUND 1

| Hole | 1 | 2 | 3 | 4 | 5 | 6 | 7 | 8 | 9 | Out | 10 | 11 | 12 | 13 | 14 | 15 | 16 | 17 | 18 | In | Total |
|------|---|---|---|---|---|---|---|---|---|-----|-----|-----|-----|-----|-----|-----|-----|-----|-----|------|-------|
| Yards | 375 | 452 | 398 | 480 | 570 | 414 | 371 | 174 | 352 | 3586 | 386 | 174 | 348 | 465 | 614 | 455 | 418 | 495 | 356 | 3711 | 7297 |
| Par | 4 | 4 | 4 | 4 | 5 | 4 | 4 | 3 | 4 | 36 | 4 | 3 | 4 | 4 | 5 | 4 | 4 | 4 | 4 | 36 | 72 |
| Score | 4 | 3 | 3 | 4 | 3 | 4 | 4 | 3 | 3 | 31 | 3 | 3 | 4 | 4 | 4 | 4 | 4 | 4 | 4 | 34 | 65 |

Signature of Marker  Hideki Matsuyama

Signature of Competitor  Dustin Johnson

*Paul Lawrie revived memories of the 1999 victory with seven birdies in a 66.*

the home honours with a round of seven birdies and only one bogey, at the 17th. The 46-year-old from Aberdeen, the 1999 Champion, admitted he had been inspired by playing with Arnold Palmer in the Champion Golfers' Challenge the previous day.

Willett matched the inward best of 33 for his second nine. He and Zach Johnson were the only two from the afternoon starters to get as high up the leaderboard. Johnson, like his namesake, was six under par after 10 and then parred in until, like so many before, finishing 5-3.

Johnson had not previously broken 70 on the Old Course, having missed the cut in 2005 — he missed the cut at each of his first three Open appearances but not since — and finished last of those who played four rounds in 2010. But the 39-year-old's Open record was certainly trending in the right direction. He was ninth at Royal Lytham & St Annes in 2012, when an opening 65 had him one off the lead, as here, and was sixth at Muirfield the following year when he topped the leaderboard on day one after a 66.

He was shocked to be able to drive the 10th green, wind-assisted, but the strength of his game is his putting and nothing settled him down more than holing a 10-footer on the first green. "That kept me composed and off to a good start playing free golf," he said. "I love this kind of golf and the more I play, the more I realise what it demands out of me."

Playing his game, and not anyone else's, would be a fine maxim for the week.

*Sergio Garcia recovers from the rough at the fourth on the way to an opening 70.*

*Robert Streb posted a 66 on his Open debut.*

*Double US Open winner Retief Goosen was also on 66.*

## FIRST ROUND LEADERS

| HOLE | 1 | 2 | 3 | 4 | 5 | 6 | 7 | 8 | 9 | 10 | 11 | 12 | 13 | 14 | 15 | 16 | 17 | 18 | TOTAL |
|---|---|---|---|---|---|---|---|---|---|---|---|---|---|---|---|---|---|---|---|
| PAR | 4 | 4 | 4 | 4 | 5 | 4 | 4 | 3 | 4 | 3 | 4 | 3 | 4 | 5 | 4 | 4 | 4 | 4 | TOTAL |
| Dustin Johnson | 4 | 3 | 3 | 4 | 3 | 4 | 4 | 3 | 3 | 3 | 3 | 3 | 4 | 4 | 4 | 4 | 4 | 4 | 65 |
| Robert Streb | 3 | 4 | 3 | 4 | 4 | 3 | 4 | 3 | 3 | 5 | 3 | 3 | 4 | 5 | 3 | 4 | 4 | 4 | 66 |
| Retief Goosen | 3 | 3 | 5 | 4 | 4 | 4 | 2 | 4 | 3 | 3 | 3 | 3 | 4 | 5 | 4 | 4 | 4 | 3 | 66 |
| Paul Lawrie | 4 | 3 | 4 | 4 | 4 | 3 | 3 | 3 | 3 | 4 | 3 | 3 | 5 | 5 | 4 | 4 | 5 | 4 | 66 |
| Jason Day | 4 | 3 | 4 | 4 | 4 | 3 | 4 | 3 | 4 | 3 | 4 | 4 | 4 | 4 | 4 | 4 | 4 | 4 | 66 |
| Zach Johnson | 3 | 3 | 4 | 4 | 4 | 3 | 4 | 3 | 3 | 3 | 3 | 4 | 4 | 4 | 5 | 4 | 5 | 3 | 66 |
| Danny Willett | 3 | 3 | 3 | 4 | 5 | 4 | 4 | 3 | 4 | 2 | 4 | 4 | 3 | 5 | 4 | 4 | 4 | 3 | 66 |

■ EAGLE OR BETTER ■ BIRDIES ■ BOGEYS ■ DBL BOGEYS/WORSE

## SCORING SUMMARY

### FIRST ROUND SCORES

| | |
|---|---|
| Players Under Par | 63 |
| Players At Par | 23 |
| Players Over Par | 70 |

### LOW SCORES

**Low First Nine**

| | |
|---|---|
| David Lingmerth | 29 |

**Low Second Nine**

| | |
|---|---|
| Retief Goosen | 33 |
| Jason Day | 33 |
| Danny Willett | 33 |
| Kevin Na | 33 |
| Matt Jones | 33 |

**Low Round**

| | |
|---|---|
| Dustin Johnson | 65 |

## FIRST ROUND HOLE SUMMARY

| HOLE | PAR | YARDS | EAGLES | BIRDIES | PARS | BOGEYS | D.BOGEYS | OTHER | RANK | AVERAGE |
|---|---|---|---|---|---|---|---|---|---|---|
| 1 | 4 | 375 | 0 | 45 | 95 | 15 | 1 | 0 | 13 | 3.821 |
| 2 | 4 | 452 | 0 | 32 | 107 | 14 | 3 | 0 | 11 | 3.923 |
| 3 | 4 | 398 | 0 | 50 | 94 | 12 | 0 | 0 | 16 | 3.756 |
| 4 | 4 | 480 | 0 | 8 | 110 | 35 | 3 | 0 | 5 | 4.212 |
| 5 | 5 | 570 | 3 | 84 | 56 | 13 | 0 | 0 | 18 | 4.506 |
| 6 | 4 | 414 | 0 | 61 | 89 | 6 | 0 | 0 | 17 | 3.647 |
| 7 | 4 | 371 | 0 | 44 | 100 | 12 | 0 | 0 | 14 | 3.795 |
| 8 | 3 | 174 | 0 | 20 | 123 | 11 | 2 | 0 | 9 | 2.968 |
| 9 | 4 | 352 | 0 | 32 | 114 | 9 | 1 | 0 | 12 | 3.865 |
| OUT | 36 | 3,586 | 3 | 376 | 888 | 127 | 10 | 0 | | 34.494 |
| 10 | 4 | 386 | 3 | 47 | 88 | 15 | 3 | 0 | 14 | 3.795 |
| 11 | 3 | 174 | 0 | 22 | 94 | 37 | 3 | 0 | 7 | 3.135 |
| 12 | 4 | 348 | 0 | 25 | 109 | 20 | 1 | 1 | 8 | 4.000 |
| 13 | 4 | 465 | 0 | 12 | 90 | 46 | 6 | 2 | 2 | 4.333 |
| 14 | 5 | 614 | 0 | 29 | 85 | 32 | 9 | 1 | 6 | 5.154 |
| 15 | 4 | 455 | 0 | 8 | 105 | 39 | 3 | 1 | 4 | 4.256 |
| 16 | 4 | 418 | 0 | 10 | 105 | 31 | 8 | 2 | 3 | 4.276 |
| 17 | 4 | 495 | 0 | 0 | 54 | 84 | 12 | 6 | 1 | 4.833 |
| 18 | 4 | 356 | 0 | 25 | 113 | 17 | 1 | 0 | 10 | 3.962 |
| IN | 36 | 3,711 | 3 | 178 | 843 | 321 | 46 | 13 | | 37.744 |
| TOTAL | 72 | 7,297 | 6 | 554 | 1,731 | 448 | 56 | 13 | | 72.237 |

_❝ If DJ keeps driving it the way he is, then I'm going to have to play my best golf to have a chance.❞_

—Jordan Spieth

_❝ I never think or wish for bad weather. I don't think any golfer does, to be fair. I have actually won tournaments in nice weather, not just bad weather, so it doesn't matter what comes. I don't wish for it. But when it does come, there's not much you can do about it.❞_

—Paul Lawrie

_❝ Tiger is why I chased the dream of becoming a professional. I saw him struggle once before and he got back to No 1. So I know he can get out of this.❞_

—Jason Day

_❝ There's an unbelievable amount of world class players playing this week so I'm not even thinking about Sunday. Right now I'm thinking about my lunch. I'm pretty hungry.❞_

—Danny Willett

_❝ I put the ball out of bounds. I three-putted, then did it again. You don't follow up an error with another error. I knew I had to hit some quality shots and I didn't. That's the disappointment — I didn't finish the deal.❞_

—Tom Watson

_❝ I have not had a meat pie yet, but my caddie has been on my case about trying one.❞_

—Robert Streb

# Spieth sticks to his game plan

*Lewine Mair follows the young American star's quest for a Grand Slam*

Forget all the hoo-ha concerning whether Jordan Spieth had been wise to play in the John Deere Classic while so many of his rivals were sharpening their links game in the Scottish Open at Gullane in the week before The Open.

The man at the centre of the debate simply steered clear of the fuss. Indeed when, in the wake of his opening 67, he was asked, "Do you think too much was made of not getting here early and all that stuff," he had the perfect riposte. "I didn't know," he said mischievously, "that there was any of 'that stuff.'"

Those who had filled column inches on how Spieth had walked the Old Course just the once, and only played it on a simulator, enjoyed the moment. Spieth had never really been in two minds as to how best to approach the third leg of his quest for a Grand Slam of all four Majors.

Though he would say at his opening press conference at St Andrews, "More time on this course couldn't ever hurt anybody," he was confident that his win at the John Deere event had been the right springboard for the week ahead.

He had wanted "to feel the pressure over the weekend" and that is what he did, coming from four back with six to play to seize the title. Simultaneously, he was able to set out for Scotland with a good idea

of what fine-tuning was required. Essentially, he needed to polish everything from his 3-iron to his driver — and to hang fast to the feel he had with his short game.

"I love where my putter is at the moment," he added, his statement all honesty as opposed to arrogance.

There were so many areas where Spieth's thinking could — and should — have been lapped up by those youngsters coming up behind him.

His attitude towards the Scottish weather? "I think it's fun. We don't come over here to get good weather. If that's what we wanted, we'd play in California. We come over here because we want to embrace the conditions."

No more was the Masters and US Open Champion expecting a succession of good bounces over the hallowed humps and hollows. "Of course you're going to get some shots that you hit good that may kick into a pot bunker," he said knowingly. "It's how do you handle that adversity and rebound quickly?"

Every great player aims to peak in the week of a Major and Spieth mentioned how his diet comes into the equation. He said he always plays better and feels better when he is at his optimum weight: "It's not like boxing or anything, but it certainly helps if I'm at full strength and have enough stamina."

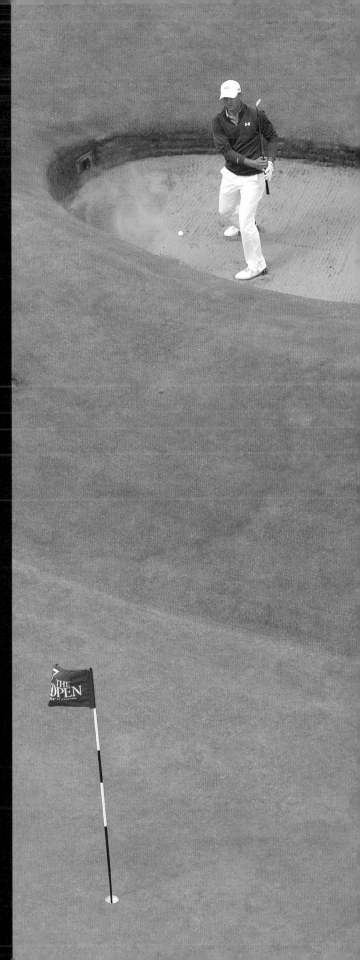

Over the week, there were other media questions which Spieth clearly saw as a tad unnecessary. Firstly, the one relating to how his first-round 67 had been a couple more than Dustin Johnson's opener. Did he think he could still beat him?

"If I didn't," he said, without the equivalent of a practice swing in which to gather his thoughts, "I would walk off and take a flight home tomorrow."

On a slightly different tack, he did not want to linger on possible parallels between himself and Tiger Woods. To him, they were too far removed from reality to be worth discussing: He would have to accomplish a great deal more before his career and Tiger's could stand comparison.

And then there was a repeat of that oft-aired query as to whether he was bound to change amid his fame and fortune. Here, he ventured to suggest that he could see no reason for anything about him, and those around him, to change. They seemed to be doing fine as they were.

So fine that Spieth would come within the proverbial whisker of winning at St Andrews. So often did his bounce-back mentality come into play, there was no writing him off, ever. Though he followed his good start with a second round in which he three-putted five times, he returned to the fray with an inward 32 for a third-round 66 which made him a real danger on a crowded 54-hole leaderboard.

In all, there would be six occasions out of nine when he responded to a mistake with a birdie. And in the case of that lone double-bogey in the final round, when the first of four putts at the short eighth hurried off the green, he made the requisite adjustment by balancing the ledger with back-to-back birdies at the next two holes.

Just when something of a miracle was required, up Spieth popped again to hole that unlikely 50-footer at the 16th. Only a 5-4 finish, instead of the necessary 4-4, finally scuppered his dream.

There would be no self-indulgent sign-off from the 21-year-old American about what might have been. His putting might not have been at its best, but he was understandably proud of the way he had battled over the course of the extended week.

"Whoever comes out the Champion," he said, without so much as a hint of wistfulness, "that's a hell of a Major."

# Time to Say Goodbye

*By Andy Farrell*

For all the trials and tribulations that had to be endured through a twice-delayed, two-day second round at the 144TH Open that saw Dustin Johnson retain his lead, there were moments of a historical nature that will live long in the memory. It was time for Tom Watson to say goodbye to the Championship, while Sir Nick Faldo also made an impromptu possible farewell.

For Watson, this was known as he arrived at St Andrews for his 38th Open on the 40th anniversary of his first victory at Carnoustie. He thought he had said farewell to the Old Course five years earlier, late on another Friday night as it happened, but The R&A extended his exemption for finishing in the top 10 in 2009 for an extra year to give the 65-year-old one last hurrah.

*Tom Watson has a moment of contemplation on the Swilcan Bridge during his final Open round.*

When he teed-off at the first the grandstands were still full and everyone rose as one to applaud. "The fans were so appreciative," Watson said, "and their applause made me feel very humble."

On and on the ovations went, but time was running out along with the daylight. Due to the morning delay because of flooding, it was touch-and-go whether his group would get finished. On the 17th tee Watson, Ernie Els and Brandt Snedeker had a discussion and made the only decision they could: to continue. A 6 at the 17th may have cost Snedeker the chance to make the cut, it really was pretty dark by now with play officially suspended at 9.54pm, but he earned the thanks of not just Watson but all those who came out to salute the five-time Champion.

On the Swilcan Bridge, after all the photographs, Watson looked skywards and thought of all the loved ones watching from upon high, former caddies Alfie Fyles and Bruce Edwards among them.

It was a cold, blustery evening and the grandstands had long since emptied except for the hardiest of perennials, something that made the scene all the more poignant. For those watching had made the effort to come back, from the pubs and restau-

*Sir Nick Faldo donned the sweater from his 1987 victory for his walk up the 18th fairway.*

rants in town; and from the temporary city under canvas they came out of the hospitality units and the media centre; and from the sanctuary of their clubhouse, Royal and Ancient Golf Club members spilled out to line the first tee. There was more applause, there were hugs, handshakes and a bow, and three cheers went up.

There were tears but not from the man himself. "Not a single one," Watson said. "My son, Michael, almost cried on the 18th tee when I said 'No tears.' But no, there weren't. It's all joy. There's no reason to be sad. I played golf for a living and played it pretty well at times. It's been a heck of a ride."

Faldo's farewell earlier in the afternoon was more spontaneous. He had muttered about going to Royal Troon or Royal Birkdale in coming years, as Sandy Lyle, 57, has the chance to do. Another

of the "Big Five" from the 1980s, Bernhard Langer, will not have the option, as he was playing as the Senior Open Champion of 2014. The German, still a full-time golfer, made the cut on the 144 mark, but Faldo, part-time golfer, full-time commentator, had no chance after the horrors of Thursday. Yet the three-time Champion stirred himself one last time. A battling 71 was capped by a birdie at the 17th which he knew was a message from the "golfing gods."

Out came his yellow Pringle sweater from Muirfield in 1987 and he stood triumphant on the Swilcan Bridge before savouring one last walk down the 18th. "That's the greatest view in golf," he said. "It looked so pretty with the stands all in R&A

---

*Jordan Spieth drives at the ninth, where a birdie awaited.*

*Flooding on the Old Course caused a suspension of play early on Friday morning.*

blue and the town, and the sun, the clouds. I'll remember that."

Some 24 hours later, when the second round was almost drawing to a conclusion, Tiger Woods said something similar to Jason Day (Louis Oosthuizen, the third member of the group, already knew how it felt to do the Champion's walk). This time Woods was bowing out early after scores of 76 and 75, missing the cut for only the second time in The Open and for the first time in successive Majors.

He received the warmest of receptions, as there was moments later for David Duval, who disappeared into something of a golfing wilderness after winning in 2001, but not this time after he made a birdie at the last to make the cut. Woods will doubtless be back at St Andrews again, but his lack of form did prompt a question about the likelihood. "It's usually every five years or so? I'll probably have less hair then and hopefully a little better game," he said.

Before leaving the 18th green, Woods told Day: "Go get it done. You know what you need to do." The Australian, on seven under par, was within striking distance of Johnson, who at 10 under par was one ahead of Danny Willett and two in front of Paul Lawrie. Alongside Day were Oosthuizen, Robert Streb, Adam Scott, Marc Warren and Zach Johnson. Everything was perfectly set up for the rest of the Championship, it had just taken longer than expected to reach the halfway point.

Torrential rain on Friday morning caused the first delay. A total of 20mm fell during the night with more than half of that in the half-hour prior to the first tee-time at 6.30am. By the time the first group got to the first green, it was under water. After some heroic squeegee work from the greens staff, play resumed at 10am with the early starters having the advantage of knowing they could finish their rounds on the day.

Willett and Zach Johnson were the first to over-

*Martin Kaymer birdies the fifth.*

*Jason Day on seven under par remained within striking distance of Dustin Johnson.*

take overnight leader Dustin Johnson. Willett got to 10 under par with his fourth birdie of the day at the 10th and, despite playing the last four holes in one over par, he set the clubhouse lead at nine under par. His scores of 66 and 69 meant that for his last 10 rounds on the Old Course, the previous eight being in the Alfred Dunhill Links Championship, he was 41 under par.

For a player who won his biggest title at the Nedbank Challenge in 2014 and had entered the world's top 50, it was still a thrill to be top of The Open leaderboard. "It's a childhood dream and looking up there it's still a bit surreal," said the 27-year-old vicar's son

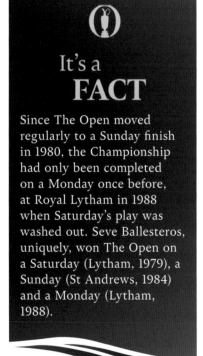

*Danny Willett just missed par at the 15th but was the Friday night clubhouse leader.*

"More junk food enthusiast than gym junkie, Daly has never been an athlete in the Dustin Johnson mould. But what he has is raw jaw-dropping talent."

—Paul Mahoney,
*The Independent*

"His own mother had somewhat underplayed her son's efforts when she sent him a text message saying, 'Well done, you've made the cut,' but Willett is very much in the hunt for the mother of all triumphs."

—Nick Rodger, *The Herald*

"As the last Englishman to win The Open, Sir Nick Faldo waved farewell to St Andrews from the Swilcan Bridge, while Danny Willett steeled himself for a weekend survival test that will determine whether he is ready to join him."

—Neil Squires, *Daily Express*

"Scott has swept into the final stages of this weather-ravaged Open with an unruffled serenity, not even dropping a stroke during a faultless second-round 67 that showcased all his links talents of lag-putting, exquisite chipping and low, raking long-irons into a gathering gale."

—Oliver Brown,
*Sunday Telegraph*

*Scotland's Marc Warren was the first player to post seven under par for 36 holes.*

from Sheffield, "but it's something I'm going to have to get used to, otherwise there's no point being up there." If he tends towards the excitable at times, his mum knew how to keep his feet on the ground, texting her congratulations "on making the cut."

Warren also posted a 69 to be seven under par, while Zach Johnson joined him on that mark after a 71. "I don't think I played much different than I did yesterday," said the American, "I just scored better yesterday and had a couple of three-putts today." Johnson admitted he feels "like I'm always under the radar," but a sign of his confidence was his statement that: "I'm excited about where my game has been and where it is right now. My outlook is to just keep doing what we're doing, trying to stay physically and mentally fresh, and enjoy the ride because this is just a lot of fun."

With the wind getting up throughout the day, Scott's bogey-free 67 was an impressive round. He was back in tandem with his old caddie, Steve Williams, and when it came to manufacturing shots to penetrate low through the breeze, the pair's discussions meant the Australian had a clear mind whatever club he committed to hitting. A good example was the "chipped" 4-iron from 196 yards at the 17th which landed short and ran up onto the green. "It came out perfect, such a small swing but a very pleasing shot, one of the best I've ever played into 17."

After his loss at Royal Lytham & St Annes in 2012, when he bogeyed the last four holes, Scott admitted he was "playing with a little bit of a chip on my shoulder." Though it got a little smaller after he won the 2013 Masters, he added: "I've been really close to lifting this trophy and I'm very motivated to do it this weekend now I'm in this position. I'd be very disappointed if I never do it in my career."

*Zach Johnson drives at the seventh. He admitted being "under the radar" but was only just below the top of the leaderboard.*

Justin Rose added a 68 to get to five under par but, in the gloaming, Luke Donald bogeyed the last two holes to fall back to six under par. On the same mark was Paul Dunne, now leading the five amateurs who made the cut, including Oliver Schniederjans who joined only Woods and Phil Mickelson since 1960 in playing all four rounds at both the US Open and The Open.

Among the 42 players who did not finish their rounds despite playing late into the increasingly blustery night was the group of Dustin Johnson, Jordan Spieth and Hideki Matsuyama. The Japanese player really sparkled as he birdied the first four holes and seven of the first 10.

A couple of shots went at the next two but he birdied the 14th as play was suspended for the night and went on to record an equal best-of-the-round 66. Johnson, just short of the green in two when he

*Two late bogeys dropped Luke Donald to six under par.*

*Louis Oosthuizen and Tiger Woods mark their balls on the 13th green as play was suspended due to strong winds.*

*Bubba Watson's Open ended with a triple-bogey at the 17th.*

elected to shut up shop, was at 10 under par, one in front of Willett and two in front of Lawrie, who had played 12 holes, and Day, who had played 11.

Throughout the night, the wind only got stronger, and when play resumed at 7am the next day only 32 minutes were possible. Officials had been out on the most exposed part of the course, the 11th green, since 6am and had not seen any balls move because of the wind. At 6.45 they determined that play would start as scheduled, but almost as soon as it did the wind increased by around 6mph. At the 11th Brooks Koepka found it difficult to replace his ball without it moving and, after finally taking one putt, impossible to do so.

Play was held up there as a higher authority was sought, while at the 14th Johnson's poor opening chip was made worse when it blew back down the bank. He made a bogey-6, while Spieth three-putted for a 5 and swished his putter angrily.

Back at the 13th Oosthuizen faced a tricky two-and-a-half footer for par but then saw it blow to within a foot of the hole. While he smiled in amazement, it then blew a further eight feet away. Then came a suspension in play that would last for 10½ hours.

Peter Dawson, Chief Executive of The R&A, explained: "When play was suspended we were experiencing average wind speeds of 25mph gusting to 40mph. Clearly, with the benefit of hindsight, it would have been better if play had not started, but the decision was taken based on the evidence at the time."

*The always popular Dunvegan Hotel drew a crowd when play was suspended during the second round.*

*Ian Poulter relaxes during Saturday's wind delay...*

*...while Jordan Spieth attempts to stay warm.*

# Up Periscope for Lawrie

Golfers are well used to delays in their profession, but the second round of the 144TH Open was a test of patience as well as golfing skill. Friday's three-and-a-quarter hour delay due to flooding was run of the mill for Marc Warren. "I had just started my warm-up so I went inside to shelter, sat in the players' lounge for 45 minutes, then ended up in the car, watching a bit of TV, 'Everybody Loves Raymond,' whatever was on, dozed on and off for a bit and was just listening to some music."

On Saturday the wind halted play at 7.32am which at least allowed players to catch up on some sleep, particularly if they were staying at the Old Course Hotel. Other sporting events kept some players happy, mostly Australians as they beat South Africa in the rugby and mauled England in the cricket.

Paul Lawrie regretted mixing it in the social media arena with Ryder Cup colleagues Ian Poulter, Lee Westwood and Darren Clarke. "My first mistake was spotting a spare seat next to them. Won't do that again," he explained.

"I'm not the best on my phone as Poulter noticed and they were taking pictures of me scratching my head. I did look as though I was a complete idiot, which probably I am with a phone to be fair.

"It was good fun and that Periscope stuff was amazing. I picked up so many followers from five minutes on there with Poulter. He loves it."

—*Andy Farrell*

*Dustin Johnson's excellent driving continued throughout a second round of 69.*

*Adam Scott and caddie Steve Williams on the 17th green following the Australian's creative approach shot.*

*American Russell Henley posted one of only two 66s.*

It was the second Open running at St Andrews where there had been a delay for wind and a debate about green speed ensued. Dawson felt a Stimpmeter reading of 10 to 10ft 6in was appropriate for the course and said: "I think what we've seen today is too strong a wind, not too fast greens."

He added: "It is also related to grass structure. We've done a lot of experimentation with the Sports Turf Research Institute into this, blowing balls on different types of grasses, although at the same Stimp reading, and you get very different results. The greens at Muirfield actually don't seem to allow the ball to blow to the degree they do here, even at comparable speeds."

According to Met Office data, St Andrews was the windiest place in Scotland, but finally the gales lessened enough to allow a 6pm resumption. Sergio Garcia immediately birdied the last two holes to reach five under par, but Bubba Watson had a triple-bogey at the 17th to miss the cut. Daniel Brooks also did not make it but had the thrill of holing his 5-iron at the 11th for a 1, having had a 40-minute wait on the tee as play got caught up.

*Hideki Matsuyama equalled the day's best round of 66 after an outward 30.*

## Round of the Day: Hideki Matsuyama – 66

**OFFICIAL SCORECARD**
**THE 144TH OPEN**
**ST ANDREWS**

Hideki MATSUYAMA
Game 43
Friday 17 July at 2:34pm

|  | FOR R&A USE ONLY 432 | ROUND 2 |
|---|---|---|
| 18 HOLE TOTAL | 72 | 36 HOLE TOTAL |
| THIS ROUND | 66 | |
| 36 HOLE TOTAL | 138 | 138 |

ROUND 2

VERIFIED

| Hole | 1 | 2 | 3 | 4 | 5 | 6 | 7 | 8 | 9 | Out |
|---|---|---|---|---|---|---|---|---|---|---|
| Yards | 375 | 452 | 398 | 480 | 570 | 414 | 371 | 174 | 352 | 3586 |
| Par | 4 | 4 | 4 | 4 | 5 | 4 | 4 | 3 | 4 | 36 |
| Score | 3 | 3 | 3 | 3 | 5 | 4 | 3 | 3 | 3 | 30 |

| Hole | 10 | 11 | 12 | 13 | 14 | 15 | 16 | 17 | 18 | In | Total |
|---|---|---|---|---|---|---|---|---|---|---|---|
| Yards | 386 | 174 | 348 | 465 | 614 | 455 | 418 | 495 | 356 | 3711 | 7297 |
| Par | 4 | 3 | 4 | 4 | 5 | 4 | 4 | 4 | 4 | 36 | 72 |
| Score | 3 | 4 | 5 | 4 | 4 | 4 | 4 | 4 | 4 | 36 | 66 |

Signature of Marker *Jordan Spieth*

Signature of Competitor *Hideki Matsuyama*
Hideki Matsuyama

"Faldo was able to offer Watson a handshake as they passed each other in a memorable snapshot of two great Open Champions in the early evening sunshine."
—Alan Pattullo, *The Scotsman*

"As the day developed, Willett was the man laying waste to the countryside and sweeping aside everyone who dared to stand in his way."
—David Facey, *The Sun*

"Like everyone, Scott woke up yesterday morning to wind and rain. Like everyone, he was glad play was suspended. Unlike everyone, he went around the links bogey-free."
—Philip Reid, *Irish Times*

"Watson's career and character have been such that you would need the emotional range of a divot not to be moved by his departure."
—Alasdair Reid, *The Times*

"The unhurried rhythm of Dustin Johnson's swing suggests a man in control of his past and, possibly, his future. He is playing near faultless golf at the moment."
—Andrew Longmore, *The Sunday Times*

*Through three days and 36 holes Dustin Johnson remained on top of the leaderboard at 10 under par.*

Oosthuizen, having stewed on his putt at the 13th all day, bravely made it and came in with a 70, as did Lawrie. Spieth had his fifth three-putt of the round at the 17th and only salvaged a 72, to stay five under par, by birdieing the last. Five behind, he was not writing himself off. "I believe I'm still in contention. I still believe I can win this tournament."

But the man in the ideal position to win was Dustin Johnson. The winners of the last five Opens at St Andrews, and of the last seven Majors generally, had all led, or shared the lead, after 36 holes. After driving the green at the 18th, Johnson posted a 69 and reflected: "I'm very pleased with my score in round two. Yesterday when we started it was difficult on the way out, then coming back in, it was even more difficult. This morning it was almost impossible, but I managed to hang in there. When we restarted just now it was very tough, but I made some good pars and then the birdie at the last. So it was a good way to finish the day."

It had been a long two days, but with a Monday finish now scheduled for the Championship, two more remained to be negotiated.

# SECOND ROUND LEADERS

| | HOLE 1 | 2 | 3 | 4 | 5 | 6 | 7 | 8 | 9 | 10 | 11 | 12 | 13 | 14 | 15 | 16 | 17 | 18 | TOTAL |
|---|---|---|---|---|---|---|---|---|---|---|---|---|---|---|---|---|---|---|---|
| PAR | 4 | 4 | 4 | 4 | 5 | 4 | 4 | 3 | 4 | 4 | 3 | 4 | 4 | 5 | 4 | 4 | 4 | 4 | TOTAL |
| Dustin Johnson | 4 | 4 | 4 | 3 | 4 | 4 | 3 | 3 | 4 | 3 | 4 | 4 | 4 | 6 | 4 | 4 | 4 | 3 | 69-134 |
| Danny Willett | 4 | 3 | 4 | 4 | 4 | 4 | 4 | 3 | 3 | 3 | 3 | 3 | 4 | 5 | 5 | 4 | 5 | 3 | 69-135 |
| Paul Lawrie | 4 | 4 | 3 | 5 | 5 | 4 | 3 | 3 | 4 | 3 | 3 | 4 | 4 | 5 | 4 | 4 | 4 | 4 | 70-136 |
| Marc Warren | 4 | 4 | 4 | 3 | 4 | 4 | 3 | 4 | 4 | 3 | 4 | 4 | 4 | 5 | 4 | 4 | 4 | 3 | 69-137 |
| Zach Johnson | 4 | 4 | 4 | 4 | 4 | 3 | 4 | 3 | 4 | 4 | 4 | 5 | 3 | 5 | 5 | 4 | 4 | 3 | 71-137 |
| Adam Scott | 4 | 4 | 4 | 4 | 4 | 4 | 4 | 3 | 3 | 4 | 2 | 3 | 4 | 5 | 4 | 4 | 4 | 3 | 67-137 |
| Robert Streb | 4 | 4 | 3 | 4 | 5 | 4 | 4 | 3 | 4 | 4 | 3 | 4 | 5 | 5 | 5 | 4 | 4 | 3 | 71-137 |
| Jason Day | 3 | 5 | 4 | 4 | 5 | 4 | 3 | 3 | 3 | 4 | 3 | 5 | 5 | 5 | 4 | 4 | 3 | | 71-137 |
| Louis Oosthuizen | 4 | 4 | 4 | 5 | 4 | 4 | 3 | 3 | 3 | 4 | 3 | 4 | 4 | 6 | 3 | 4 | 4 | 4 | 70-137 |

**■ EAGLE OR BETTER    ■ BIRDIES    ■ BOGEYS    ■ DBL BOGEYS/WORSE**

# SCORING SUMMARY

## SECOND ROUND SCORES

| | |
|---|---|
| Players Under Par | 59 |
| Players At Par | 25 |
| Players Over Par | 72 |

## LOW SCORES

**Low First Nine**
| | |
|---|---|
| Hideki Matsuyama | 30 |

**Low Second Nine**
| | |
|---|---|
| Sergio Garcia | 32 |
| Ryan Fox | 32 |

**Low Round**
| | |
|---|---|
| Hideki Matsuyama | 66 |
| Russell Henley | 66 |

# SECOND ROUND HOLE SUMMARY

| HOLE | PAR | YARDS | EAGLES | BIRDIES | PARS | BOGEYS | D.BOGEYS | OTHER | RANK | AVERAGE |
|---|---|---|---|---|---|---|---|---|---|---|
| 1 | 4 | 375 | 0 | 25 | 116 | 12 | 3 | 0 | 11 | 3.955 |
| 2 | 4 | 452 | 0 | 13 | 102 | 40 | 0 | 1 | 4 | 4.192 |
| 3 | 4 | 398 | 0 | 28 | 113 | 13 | 2 | 0 | 12 | 3.929 |
| 4 | 4 | 480 | 0 | 15 | 101 | 37 | 3 | 0 | 5 | 4.179 |
| 5 | 5 | 570 | 3 | 75 | 70 | 8 | 0 | 0 | 17 | 4.532 |
| 6 | 4 | 414 | 1 | 18 | 114 | 21 | 2 | 0 | 10 | 4.032 |
| 7 | 4 | 371 | 0 | 36 | 112 | 8 | 0 | 0 | 16 | 3.821 |
| 8 | 3 | 174 | 0 | 16 | 114 | 22 | 4 | 0 | 8 | 3.090 |
| 9 | 4 | 352 | 0 | 31 | 109 | 14 | 2 | 0 | 13 | 3.917 |
| OUT | 36 | 3,586 | 4 | 257 | 951 | 175 | 16 | 1 | | 35.647 |
| 10 | 4 | 386 | 0 | 38 | 99 | 18 | 0 | 1 | 14 | 3.891 |
| 11 | 3 | 174 | 1 | 9 | 83 | 60 | 3 | 0 | 2 | 3.353 |
| 12 | 4 | 348 | 0 | 18 | 105 | 30 | 3 | 0 | 7 | 4.115 |
| 13 | 4 | 465 | 0 | 15 | 104 | 36 | 1 | 0 | 6 | 4.147 |
| 14 | 5 | 614 | 1 | 47 | 82 | 25 | 0 | 1 | 15 | 4.865 |
| 15 | 4 | 455 | 0 | 19 | 112 | 24 | 1 | 0 | 9 | 4.045 |
| 16 | 4 | 418 | 0 | 6 | 115 | 27 | 5 | 3 | 3 | 4.256 |
| 17 | 4 | 495 | 0 | 6 | 75 | 64 | 9 | 2 | 1 | 4.526 |
| 18 | 4 | 356 | 0 | 80 | 72 | 4 | 0 | 0 | 18 | 3.513 |
| IN | 36 | 3,711 | 2 | 238 | 847 | 288 | 22 | 7 | | 36.712 |
| TOTAL | 72 | 7,297 | 6 | 495 | 1,798 | 463 | 38 | 8 | | 72.359 |

" I told my son there should be no crying. Let's enjoy the walk up the final hole. "

—Tom Watson

" I just had a text message off my mum saying, 'Well done, you've made the cut'. Thanks mum, bring me back down to earth. "

—Danny Willett

" It's for The Open. I'll stay until it's done. "

—Louis Oosthuizen

" This is something everyone dreams about who's played golf as a kid. To live out at least a part of that dream is pretty cool. "

—Marc Warren

" I kind of feel like I'm always under the radar. "

—Zach Johnson

" I feel I have been really close to lifting this trophy and I am very motivated now I'm in this position. You know, I think I'm playing with a little bit of a chip on my shoulder. "

—Adam Scott

" There's 36 holes to go. There's a lot of world class players in there. If you start getting ahead of yourself, you start making mistakes and tripping up. All I'm thinking about is getting on the first tee on Sunday, picking my line and making a good swing. "

—Paul Lawrie

" If I can shoot something like 10 under in the last two rounds, I still think I'll have a chance to win. "

# A Pringle farewell for Faldo

*Peter Dixon watches the six-time Major winner enjoy the perfect send-off.*

If any of today's young players were to ask what was so special about Sir Nick Faldo in his prime, by way of illustration you could point them in the direction of his cameo performance in the second round of the 144ᵀᴴ Open.

At his peak Faldo was unyielding, single-minded, and intense. His never-say-die attitude intimidated rivals and spoke volumes for the man. He was undaunted, unfearing, unshakeable. And it is why he lifted three Claret Jugs and donned three Green Jackets in a stellar career during which he became the game's pre-eminent force.

So when it came to bidding a final farewell to The Open — where better than at the Home of Golf and the scene of his record-breaking victory a quarter of a century earlier? — the most successful British golfer of the modern era dug deep inside himself to bring

to the surface a nugget of gold that had lain hidden for years. A day before his 58th birthday, Faldo was determined not to go out with a whimper.

In the first round, though, he had looked every inch the part-time golfer, someone who now spends most of his time in the television commentary box, observing others and passing comment. Playing alongside Justin Rose and Rickie Fowler, Faldo was not even a shadow of his former self. Eight bogeys and a triple left him propping up the field with an 11-over-par 83. This was not so much a swansong as a dirge — and, for Faldo, it simply would not do.

The second round was an altogether different story. A one-under-par 71 that included a birdie at the fearsome 17th, courtesy of a 20-foot putt from off the green (above), showed Faldo at his obdurate best.

Pride was at stake and they come no prouder than the six times Major Champion.

In fact the round almost never happened. In a freak accident earlier in the week, Faldo had cut the middle finger of his right hand when he caught it on deer antlers mounted to the wall of his rented house. The wound required constant attention and when Friday came around the cut had opened up again and he needed further hospital treatment. Had it not been for a three-hour weather delay, he would probably have missed his tee-time.

"I went back to the hospital and had it glued and I didn't know what I wanted to do," Faldo recalled. "And then the kids looked at me and said, 'Dad, what are we doing?' And I said, 'I don't know.' They said, 'We think you should go play.' When your kids say you're going, you're going.

"That was the goal of the week. The goal was to stand on the Swilcan Bridge and get the picture. I knew I was bringing this thing" — the sweater he had worn in winning The Open for the first time, at Muirfield in 1987 — "bust out my ol' Pringle, so I knew I was doing that. That was the image of the week."

At the 16th Faldo passed Tom Watson, five times an Open Champion and also playing the Old Course for the last time, coming the other way. The handshake between the two could not have been more fitting: it represented the passing of time, the moving on of two great Champions.

For Faldo, however, there was still one last hurrah as he moved ever closer to the town. He had desperately wanted to put on a show for his friends and family, for his son Matthew, who was caddying for him, and for the thousands of fans around the course. In truth, the birdie at the Road Hole was beyond his wildest dreams. The gods had been good to him over the years, however, and they were to give him one final glorious moment in the sun, a rainbow appearing in the distance as he sank the most improbable of birdie putts.

"How could I do that?" Faldo asked. "I think I've only done it twice — last round 10 years ago. That's why I looked to the gods, the St Andrews golfing gods. I thought, 'Thank you very much for that.' I felt beat up yesterday, but that was one of the great moments of my career, making a 3 there and walking the walk."

The walk, of course, was to the Swilcan Bridge after he had teed-off at the 18th, a hole he was subsequently to par. As if by magic, the old yellow sweater appeared and there he stood, arms aloft, tears in his eyes, and deservedly milking the applause of the galleries. He was joined at one stage by his playing partners and his son, but the pictures of him in splendid isolation most captured the essence of Faldo, the player and the man.

It was the perfect setting for the perfect send-off. Except for one small hint from Faldo himself. "If I'm sensible, that's it," he said. "I'll do my best to be sensible."

## THE OPEN

### THIRD ROUND
19 July 2015

# Sunday Cheer for Dunne

*By Andy Farrell*

This was the day the 144TH Open came to life. It was one of the great Sundays in the Championship's history and there was the bonus of a day still to come.

And what a final day there was in prospect. A crowded leaderboard that offered 14 players within three strokes of the lead, half of them Major winners, contained many potential stories.

The most obvious of them blazing down from the electronic scoreboards included Jordan Spieth's quest for the Grand Slam being alive again. Or could Louis Oosthuizen win a second St Andrews Open in a row, or Padraig Harrington a third Claret Jug? Could Adam Scott redeem himself after coming so close at Royal Lytham & St Annes? What about Jason Day finally succeeding after his health issues, or Marc Leishman after his wife's frightening near-fatal illness? Or Sergio Garcia after, well, just years of trying and hoping? Would Retief Goosen or Zach Johnson add to their previous Majors won in the

*An amateur leads The Open — Paul Dunne tied at the top.*

States? Could a Brit do it? In which case Justin Rose or Danny Willett were your men.

Yet most tantalising of all, for it was so unexpected, was the prospect of an amateur lifting the Claret Jug for the first time in 85 years. This had not happened since Bobby Jones won at Royal Liverpool in 1930. And not since 1927, here at St Andrews, had an amateur led after 54 holes. But now Paul Dunne was leading The Open.

And the Irishman was not the only amateur managing to turn the hunt for the Silver Medal into something bigger entirely. American Jordan Niebrugge scored his second 67 of the week to join the group on nine under par that included the likes of Rose and Garcia, Scott and Goosen, Johnson and Willett.

But Dunne produced a 66 that eclipsed all the other wonderful performances on show this day. At 12 under par the 22-year-old from Greystones was sharing the lead with Oosthuizen and Day, one ahead of Spieth and two in front of his distinguished compatriot Harrington.

His round bettered the amateur record for an Open at St Andrews of 67 first set by Joe Carr in 1960 and equalled twice by Niebrugge this week.

*Jason Day shared the 54-hole lead as he did at the US Open a month earlier.*

His total of 204 smashed by six the previous best by an amateur after 54 holes, first set by Iain Pyman at Royal St George's in 1993. And given his opening pair of 69s, he was the first amateur to record his first three rounds in the 60s.

Yet it was the manner of his performance that so captured the imagination of everyone watching outside the ropes and earned admiration from those competing against him inside them. Day admitted to knowing "absolutely nothing" about Dunne, but having watched from the pairing behind all the way round the Old Course, the Australian was won over.

"He's playing fantastic golf," Day said. "He looks like a veteran though he looks very young. But the way he goes about his process, he looks like he's very present. He obviously played with Louis and to be able to play the way he did with the last winner of the Open Championship here, on a big stage, especially Sunday with a lot of people watching, was pretty special."

"He played unbelievable golf," confirmed Oosthuizen, who was startled by the quality of Dunne's second shot at the 17th, a beautiful 4-iron from 220 yards that finished 20 feet from the hole. "That second shot into 17 was one of the best I've seen," said the South

*Charl Schwartzel tangled with the Swilcan Burn and made a bogey at the first hole.*

*Louis Oosthuizen, after a birdie at the last to tie for the lead, congratulates Dunne for his play.*

*Rickie Fowler scored a 66 but was still five behind.*

African. "He made me so nervous on my second shot because I was going to play a completely different shot, low, running up there, and tugged it a little to the left. His was an amazing shot. He deserved to birdie that."

But the putt refused to drop, one of the few things that did not work out on this special day. From the start it had gone so well. He hit a wedge to two feet at the first for a 3 and birdied the fourth and the seventh, where he holed a 50-footer from off the green. A pair of 3s at the ninth and 10th meant he broke out of a six-way tie for the lead, a measure of how bunched the leaderboard had got, to sit one ahead of the entire field.

That did not last, but Dunne in no way looked overawed or out of place on the run for home. A 20-footer at the 15th gave him a sixth birdie and he kept producing quality shots that thrilled the galleries. Now the autograph hunters would be

*A Sunday 65 left Padraig Harrington in fifth place.*

seeking him out, rather than mistaking him for the man of the moment, Spieth.

"I had so much support from the crowd, they kept me lifted the whole way through," he said. "Every shot I hit was getting cheered from start to finish. And it was great to play with Louis Oosthuizen. He's a great player, someone I look up to, a great role model. He was a really nice playing partner and I really enjoyed it. It was a fun day."

Dunne, who won the Final Qualifying event at Woburn for the second year running, had a clear game plan. "I went out there thinking that if I could play sensibly and keep the bogeys off my card, you're going to have so many opportunities for birdie that you are bound to make some. I was really pleased to keep the bogeys off the card today."

In fact, through 54 holes, Dunne had only lapsed over par twice, the least of anyone in the field. These

*Adam Scott leaves an approach putt short at the seventh.*

# Happens to the best

Rarely has a player experienced quite such a range of emotions so quickly as Eddie Pepperell late in his third round. One minute the 24-year-old Englishman, playing in his first Open, had collected his eighth birdie of the day with a brilliant putt at the 16th, the next he had hit into the Old Course Hotel.

It is the sort of worst nightmare that plagues any handicap golfer standing on the 17th tee. But it rarely happens to someone leading The Open as Pepperell was after tying Dustin Johnson at 10 under par.

Not that he knew it. He was just excited about his play. "I felt really confident coming off 16," he said. "Holing that putt was really good and maybe the tee shot was down to a little bit of complacency, not focusing on the right things in my routine.

"But this is golf. We all know how tough it is on 17, into the wind off the left, it doesn't get much tougher than that. I didn't quite master it today."

Honest and philosophical, Pepperell admitted his driving had perhaps prevented him from winning in three years on the European Tour. "How can I say this? The tee shot on 17 didn't come as a huge surprise, unfortunately it came at the wrong time."

Despite a double-bogey, he still signed for a 66 and was perhaps comforted by Phil Mickelson doing exactly the same at the 17th on Monday. It can happen to the best of them.

—Andy Farrell

were the best scoring conditions of the week, with the wind down. It allowed the early markers to go low and, first out, David Duval celebrated his first cut made at The Open since 2008 with his lowest score since he won in 2001, matching his final-day 67.

Eddie Pepperell and amateur Ashley Chesters both rushed to the turn in 31, but it was Leishman who produced the day's lowest round, a 64 that could have been even lower. Starting at one under par, the 31-year-old Australian had pars at each of the first three holes then birdied eight of the next 12. There were 2s at each of the short holes, but he found a bunker at the 14th to miss out on a birdie-4 there, only to hole a 15-footer at the 15th. He was only one more birdie away from equalling the Major record of 63, last achieved at St Andrews by Rory McIlroy in 2010.

Leishman, who scored a 65 in the final round at Hoylake in 2014 to finish in a tie for fifth place, had a chance at the 16th which just slipped by and then an even better one at the 17th which looked for all the world as if it must go in. "I was definitely trying to make it and it did look really good," he said, having swayed up and out of his stance in surprise when the ball refused to drop.

At the last his short approach was close to being good, which at the 18th at St Andrews inevitably means it ends up in the Valley of Sin. "I gave myself some really good chances on the last three holes, so it was disappointing not to go a couple better,"

*Overnight leader Dustin Johnson, here in trouble at the 17th, bogeyed the last three holes.*

he said. "But as far as the week goes, 64 gets me right back in it."

Leishman had started the day one stroke off the cut-line and the best score of the week, as it turned out, left him at that point one behind Dustin Johnson's overnight lead. Not that Johnson stayed in the lead, his Sunday misfortunes in the Majors continuing. On a day when 63 of the 80 players scored under par, the tall American was not one of them. None of those in the last two pairings did so, and as it got cold and a little breezier later on, this summed up the pressure of leading The Open.

Scots Paul Lawrie and Marc Warren had a 74 and a 72 respectively, Willett a 72 and Johnson a 75. Willett, with three birdies in the first 10 holes, did have a moment in the lead but the Englishman then bogeyed three of the last six. Nothing much happened for Johnson. He got stuck in par mode, except for a bogey at the seventh and a birdie at

*Eddie Pepperell sees his drive at the 17th sail into the hotel.*

*Home favourite Paul Lawrie slipped down the leaderboard with a 74.*

*Sergio Garcia's putt at the 16th just misses.*

the 15th from one of the harder putts he faced. The others just refrained from dropping. "I didn't feel I played that bad," he sighed. "It's definitely frustrating." Even more so by the time he had bogeyed the last three holes.

There were 68s for Garcia, trending in the right direction after a 70 and a 69, and Rose, for the second day running, to join Leishman and Niebrugge. Harrington returned a 65 that included a holed 40-footer at the 16th. "I always wanted to shoot 65 on the Sunday of The Open, though obviously there's another round to go," joked the Irishman after he posted the new clubhouse lead at 10 under par.

Then came Spieth, who was looking miffed with life when he three-putted once again at the ninth hole. He punched his golf bag, not wanting to break a club or punch his caddie, and admitted that along with his three-putt at the 14th on Saturday morning, "Those two moments were as frustrated as I've been."

*Jordan Spieth plays his approach to the last for a thrilling 66.*

*David Duval turned back the years with a 67.*

*Danny Willett acknowledges the gallery after a 72.*

But he responded just as we have come to expect by birdieing the next three holes. There were also good par-saves at the 13th and 14th holes before another birdie at the 15th which got him home in 32. His 66, to be 11 under par, had the same effect on his rivals that a similar thrust by Tiger Woods had in his prime. They knew that having got the bug for winning Majors, Spieth did not want to stop now. "I'm not playing for a place," said the 21-year-old American. "I want to win."

As for what that win would mean, the added history, he was either not thinking about it, or thinking it could only spur him on. "If I have a chance coming down the stretch, if it creeps in,

*Martin Kaymer received plenty of German support as he studied his putt at 18.*

"Paul Dunne began this week with a profile so low it needed a miner's lamp. Now he has a chance to be the leading light at The Open Championship if he can just see off a legend-elect and a leaderboard brimming over with intricately plotted dramas."
—Rick Broadbent, *The Times*

"As thrilling as amateur kid Paul Dunne's rise to the top of the leaderboard may be, perhaps the most significant charge of the day was Jordan Spieth's remarkable back nine that leaves him lurking ominously over the shoulders of the three joint leaders."
—Euan McLean, *Daily Record*

"Moving Day moved from Saturday to Sunday after all the weather interruptions and it lived up to its moniker."
—Neil Squires, *Daily Express*

"When a shootout at St Andrews ended on Sunday, 14 players were separated by three shots. Half of them were Major Champions. Even for a place packed with centuries of history, this Open offered endless possibilities."
—Doug Ferguson, *Associated Press*

# Family first for Leishman

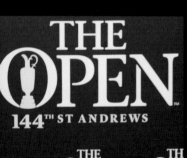

After a best-of-the-day 64 in the third round, Marc Leishman found himself just three strokes off the lead and a serious contender heading into the final day of competition. But while a first Major Championship victory was tantalisingly within reach, the Australian was only too aware that his world would not stop spinning if he eventually came up short.

Coming into the 144TH Open, Leishman carried with him a rather large dose of perspective. Less than four months earlier his wife Audrey was taken so seriously ill that doctors gave her only a five per cent chance of survival.

She had been diagnosed as having toxic-shock syndrome, a rare and often fatal bacterial infection, and was placed in a medically induced coma.

Leishman had been preparing for the Masters at the time, but now had to consider the prospect of life outside the sport as a single paren of two sons, Oliver and Harvey Thankfully, Audrey started slowly to recover and was released from hospital two weeks later, weak bu on the mend.

"It was a huge possibility that wasn't going to be playing golf any more," Leishman said. "Travelling with a one-year-old and a three-year-old by yourself isn't really — well, it wasn't going to happen

"The experience changed my perspective on life. I don't ge annoyed about little things tha I can't really help. When you hi a bad shot there's no real poin getting frustrated.

"And even if I do have a bad day I can still go home and hopefully give Audrey a hug and cuddle my boys. For a while it didn't look like I was going to be able to dc that."

—Peter Dixor

## Round of the Day: **Marc Leishman – 64**

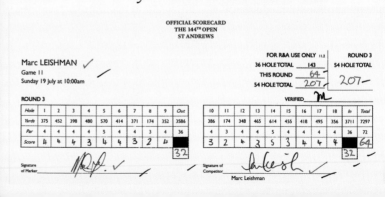

OFFICIAL SCORECARD
THE 144TH OPEN
ST ANDREWS

Marc LEISHMAN ✓
Game 11
Sunday 19 July at 10:00am

| | FOR R&A USE ONLY 11.2 | ROUND 3 |
|---|---|---|
| 36 HOLE TOTAL | 143 | 54 HOLE TOTAL |
| THIS ROUND | 64 | |
| 54 HOLE TOTAL | 207 | 207 |
| VERIFIED | M | |

**ROUND 3**

| Hole | 1 | 2 | 3 | 4 | 5 | 6 | 7 | 8 | 9 | Out |
|---|---|---|---|---|---|---|---|---|---|---|
| Yards | 375 | 452 | 398 | 480 | 570 | 414 | 371 | 174 | 352 | 3586 |
| Par | 4 | 4 | 4 | 4 | 5 | 4 | 4 | 3 | 4 | 36 |
| Score | 4 | 4 | 4 | 3 | 4 | 4 | 3 | 2 | 4 | 32 |

| Hole | 10 | 11 | 12 | 13 | 14 | 15 | 16 | 17 | 18 | In | Total |
|---|---|---|---|---|---|---|---|---|---|---|---|
| Yards | 386 | 174 | 348 | 465 | 614 | 455 | 418 | 495 | 356 | 3711 | 7297 |
| Par | 4 | 3 | 4 | 4 | 5 | 4 | 4 | 4 | 4 | 36 | 72 |
| Score | 3 | 2 | 4 | 3 | 5 | 3 | 4 | 4 | 4 | 32 | 64 |

Signature of Marker

Signature of Competitor

Marc Leishman

*A pot of gold awaiting someone? The scene on Sunday evening at close of play.*

I'll embrace the opportunity that presents itself," he insisted. "Why should it add more pressure in a negative way? If it adds more pressure, it just makes me feel this is something that's a little more special. But I need to manage that, and while I recognise what is at stake, I need to simplify things and just go about my business."

Both Oosthuizen and Day scored 67s. The South African had a couple of bogeys and needed to finish with three birdies in the last five holes, including at the last, just to keep up with his playing partner, young Dunne. Day went bogey-free to reward his patience on a day when the danger was to "look at the leaderboard and try and chase it by forcing the birdies."

Day had a chance to take the solo lead at the last but had to settle for a par. An omen perhaps for the following day? As much as he knew that only by putting himself in contention time and again will a first Major title arrive, Day also noted: "You can't count the guys behind us out. It's too bunched. Everyone is going to be excited about how it pans out. It should be fun."

Slightly out of the limelight, with everything else going on, Scott and Zach Johnson, thanks to a 3-5-3 finish, returned a pair of 70s to join those on nine under par. Earlier, Leishman had said he learned a lot from playing with Scott in the final round of the 2013 Masters.

Johnson had played alongside Ernie Els at Royal Lytham in 2012. "I got to witness what it takes to win from behind," he recalled. "It was cool to see what he was doing. You never know."

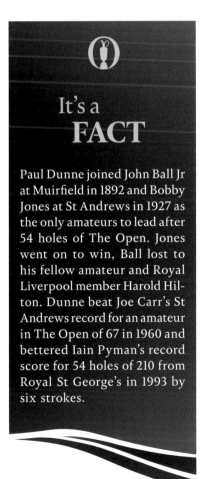

It's a
**FACT**

Paul Dunne joined John Ball Jr at Muirfield in 1892 and Bobby Jones at St Andrews in 1927 as the only amateurs to lead after 54 holes of The Open. Jones went on to win, Ball lost to his fellow amateur and Royal Liverpool member Harold Hilton. Dunne beat Joe Carr's St Andrews record for an amateur in The Open of 67 in 1960 and bettered Iain Pyman's record score for 54 holes of 210 from Royal St George's in 1993 by six strokes.

> *It's surreal I'm leading The Open. If we were playing an amateur event here, I wouldn't be too surprised by the scores I shot. It's just lucky that it happens to be in the biggest event in the world.*
>
> —Paul Dunne

> *This course is soft and it's taking on a lot of good scores, so it's surprising the leaders didn't really get it going today. But that's the pressure of The Open.*
>
> —Adam Scott

> *At this point it's free rolling. I'm going to play to win. I'm not playing for a place.*
>
> —Jordan Spieth

> *I always wanted to be the first Aussie to win the Masters, but Scottie beat me to it. As we haven't had an Aussie win the Claret Jug since Mr Norman, it would be nice to put my name on the Jug. We're just trying to chase that bit of immortality.*
>
> —Jason Day

> *As Australians we grew up watching Greg Norman win The Open Championship. It would be great to get a hold of that trophy and nice to take it back for Audrey and the boys.*
>
> —Marc Leishman

> *I just tried to play my game all day, and I did. I just didn't hole any putts.*
>
> —Dustin Johnson

> *Three shots back at an Open Championship is never too far back.*
>
> —Danny Willett

---

*Dunne was out of position on the fifth but did not drop a shot all day.*

## THIRD ROUND LEADERS

| HOLE | 1 | 2 | 3 | 4 | 5 | 6 | 7 | 8 | 9 | 10 | 11 | 12 | 13 | 14 | 15 | 16 | 17 | 18 | |
|---|---|---|---|---|---|---|---|---|---|---|---|---|---|---|---|---|---|---|---|
| PAR | 4 | 4 | 4 | 4 | 5 | 4 | 4 | 3 | 4 | 4 | 3 | 4 | 4 | 5 | 4 | 4 | 4 | 4 | TOTAL |
| Paul Dunne* | 3 | 4 | 4 | 3 | 5 | 4 | 3 | 3 | 3 | 3 | 3 | 4 | 4 | 5 | 3 | 4 | 4 | 4 | 66-204 |
| Louis Oosthuizen | 4 | 4 | 4 | 3 | 4 | 4 | 3 | 4 | 4 | 4 | 2 | 5 | 4 | 4 | 3 | 4 | 4 | 3 | 67-204 |
| Jason Day | 4 | 4 | 4 | 4 | 4 | 3 | 4 | 3 | 4 | 4 | 2 | 4 | 3 | 5 | 3 | 4 | 4 | 4 | 67-204 |
| Jordan Spieth | 3 | 4 | 4 | 4 | 4 | 4 | 3 | 3 | 5 | 3 | 2 | 3 | 4 | 5 | 3 | 4 | 4 | 4 | 66-205 |
| Padraig Harrington | 3 | 4 | 3 | 4 | 4 | 4 | 4 | 3 | 3 | 3 | 3 | 3 | 4 | 5 | 4 | 3 | 4 | 4 | 65-206 |

**■ EAGLE OR BETTER    ■ BIRDIES    ■ BOGEYS    ■ DBL BOGEYS/WORSE**

## SCORING SUMMARY

### THIRD ROUND SCORES

| | |
|---|---|
| Players Under Par | 63 |
| Players At Par | 6 |
| Players Over Par | 11 |

### LOW SCORES

| | |
|---|---|
| **Low First Nine** | |
| Eddie Pepperell | 31 |
| Ashley Chesters* | 31 |
| **Low Second Nine** | |
| Jordan Spieth | 32 |
| Marc Leishman | 32 |
| Ryan Palmer | 32 |
| Patrick Reed | 32 |
| **Low Round** | |
| Marc Leishman | 64 |

## THIRD ROUND HOLE SUMMARY

| HOLE | PAR | YARDS | EAGLES | BIRDIES | PARS | BOGEYS | D.BOGEYS | OTHER | RANK | AVERAGE |
|---|---|---|---|---|---|---|---|---|---|---|
| 1 | 4 | 375 | 0 | 22 | 55 | 3 | 0 | 0 | 14 | 3.763 |
| 2 | 4 | 452 | 0 | 11 | 56 | 9 | 4 | 0 | 3 | 4.075 |
| 3 | 4 | 398 | 0 | 17 | 59 | 4 | 0 | 0 | 10 | 3.838 |
| 4 | 4 | 480 | 0 | 13 | 50 | 16 | 0 | 1 | 3 | 4.075 |
| 5 | 5 | 570 | 2 | 46 | 31 | 1 | 0 | 0 | 18 | 4.388 |
| 6 | 4 | 414 | 0 | 15 | 51 | 13 | 1 | 0 | 5 | 4.000 |
| 7 | 4 | 371 | 0 | 19 | 58 | 3 | 0 | 0 | 12 | 3.800 |
| 8 | 3 | 174 | 0 | 5 | 70 | 5 | 0 | 0 | 5 | 3.000 |
| 9 | 4 | 352 | 0 | 31 | 48 | 1 | 0 | 0 | 17 | 3.625 |
| OUT | 36 | 3,586 | 2 | 179 | 478 | 55 | 5 | 1 | | 34.562 |
| 10 | 4 | 386 | 0 | 20 | 55 | 5 | 0 | 0 | 11 | 3.812 |
| 11 | 3 | 174 | 0 | 32 | 44 | 4 | 0 | 0 | 16 | 2.650 |
| 12 | 4 | 348 | 0 | 20 | 51 | 8 | 1 | 0 | 8 | 3.875 |
| 13 | 4 | 465 | 0 | 19 | 53 | 8 | 0 | 0 | 9 | 3.862 |
| 14 | 5 | 614 | 2 | 24 | 45 | 7 | 2 | 0 | 13 | 4.787 |
| 15 | 4 | 455 | 0 | 15 | 59 | 6 | 0 | 0 | 7 | 3.888 |
| 16 | 4 | 418 | 0 | 6 | 59 | 13 | 2 | 0 | 2 | 4.138 |
| 17 | 4 | 495 | 0 | 2 | 48 | 26 | 3 | 1 | 1 | 4.412 |
| 18 | 4 | 356 | 0 | 26 | 50 | 4 | 0 | 0 | 15 | 3.725 |
| IN | 36 | 3,711 | 2 | 164 | 464 | 81 | 8 | 1 | | 35.150 |
| TOTAL | 72 | 7,297 | 4 | 343 | 942 | 136 | 13 | 2 | | 69.713 |

# Amateur extras take starring roles

*Alistair Tait celebrates the strong amateur challenge at St Andrews.*

You have to go back a long way to find a third round of an Open that thrilled amateur golf aficionados the way the 144[TH] Open did — 88 years, to be precise.

Normally the amateur challenge is a minor sideshow in the bigger plot to determine the Champion Golfer of the Year. No one appeared to have told the unpaid players at St Andrews what roles they were expected to play on the game's greatest stage. Either that or they had simply refused to read the script. They were not intent on being mere extras. They wanted starring roles.

Ireland's Paul Dunne took centre stage when he fashioned a six-under-par 66 to tie for the lead on 12 under par with 2010 Champion Louis Oosthuizen and Australia's Jason Day. American Jordan Niebrugge was three shots behind on nine under par, while England's Ashley Chesters lay within six shots in equal 26th place. Former world amateur No 1 Oliver Schniederjans was on four under par, tied for 45th, with the Amateur Champion Romain Langasque also making the cut. They were among the nine amateurs who qualified for The Open.

Dunne found himself in illustrious company in the history books when the third round ended. Not since Bobby Jones in 1927 at St Andrews had an amateur held the lead in the Championship. No unpaid player had led a Major after 54 holes since Jim Simons in the 1971 US Open.

More importantly, no amateur had won The Open since Jones at Royal Liverpool in 1930, and there had been no amateur Major winner since Johnny Goodman took the US Open in 1933.

No wonder St Andrews was buzzing on the eve of the final round. Could Dunne or Niebrugge do the unthinkable? One double Major winner certainly thought so.

"I'm not extremely surprised," reigning Masters and US Open winner Jordan Spieth said. "The amateur game has changed to be more like the professional game. There are more tournaments, better golf courses, harder golf courses and better competition. That's what I felt when I was playing junior golf into amateur golf. It was almost like a mini PGA Tour.

"There will be an amateur that wins a PGA Tour event or something like that, possibly even a Major, I think, at some point in the next decade."

Dunne certainly had eyes on the biggest prize. He didn't seem content with winning the Silver Medal for low amateur. "I'm well capable of shooting the scores that I need to win if everyone else doesn't shoot their best," said the recent graduate of the University of Alabama, Birmingham.

"It's surreal that I'm leading The Open, but I can easily believe that I shot the scores I shot. If I were playing an amateur event here, I wouldn't be too surprised. It's just lucky that it happens to be in the biggest event in the world."

The Spieth factor was one reason the amateurs

*Jordan Niebrugge tied sixth.*

*Romain Langasque tied 45th.*

were contending in the game's oldest and greatest tournament.

"I think you're seeing so many amateurs playing well because we're inspired by the young guys on tour like Jordan, who aren't that much older than us," Niebrugge said.

Both Niebrugge (21) and Langasque (20) were younger than Spieth (21, almost 22), while the other three were older. Dunne and Schniederjans were a year older, while Chesters was the "old man" at 25.

Oklahoma State player Niebrugge had benefited from links experience in the run-up to St Andrews. He qualified for the match play stages of The Amateur Championship at Carnoustie and earned his spot in The Open by finishing joint leading qualifier at Hillside.

Chesters had a distinct advantage over the rest since he had played the St Andrews Links Trophy for four straight years. However, he wasn't exactly in the best frame of mind when he began his third round. "The first two days I didn't actually feel pressure, but for some reason this morning I didn't hit the ball very well on the range, which didn't help," he said. "For the first hole I was definitely a bit shaky."

It didn't take long for the nerves to dissipate, however. "I hit it close at the second and after that the nerves went," said Chesters, who birdied the second hole en route to a five-under-par 67 that put him in contention.

Schniederjans returned a third-round 70 but felt he should have been closer to the lead than 45th. "I'm hitting the ball the best in my life," he said. "If I had putted better over the last few days I'd be up near the top."

That sense of comfort among the world's elite was clearly shared by all five amateurs to have reached the third round. They weren't there just to make up the numbers.

As we know, Jones' record as the last amateur winner of The Open remains intact. Dunne didn't pull off the miracle many had hoped for. In the end it would be left to Niebrugge to flirt with history before settling for the Silver Medal.

The message Niebrugge and company sent from this Open was clear — the gulf between the best amateurs and top professionals is not as wide as people may think.

*Ashley Chesters tied 26th.*

*Paul Dunne tied 30th.*

## FOURTH ROUND
20 July 2015

# It's Zach on Manic Monday

*By Andy Farrell*

Perhaps if you take the last time there was a Monday finish in The Open and add in the last time there was a play-off at St Andrews, then you might be part of the way towards comprehending the magnitude of the events with which the 144TH version of the game's oldest Championship climaxed.

Part of the way. But it would be a good start. In 1988 at Royal Lytham when play similarly overran, we were rewarded with Seve Ballesteros triumphing in a pulsating three-way battle with the two Nicks, Price and Faldo. While 20 years ago there were Costantino Rocca's dramatics from the Valley of Sin and John Daly's eventual victory. Here the twists and turns kept coming at dizzying speed.

That slightly dazed look on the face of Zach Johnson when it became apparent that he would

*Zach Johnson celebrates his birdie at the 72nd hole to set the clubhouse target at 15 under par.*

be lifting the Claret Jug, rather than one from a myriad of others, was completely understandable. "This to me was one of the most exciting Opens," said Louis Oosthuizen, whose putt on the 18th to extend the play-off only just missed, giving victory to Johnson and finally extinguishing his own hopes of a double St Andrews victory. About the only thing this Open did not have, after an extra day and four extra holes, was sudden-death.

It just felt like it as a string of players faced enough do-or-die moments to brighten up another cool, blustery grey day — in other words ideal St Andrews conditions. A gallery of around 35,000 for this unscheduled manic Monday, with some 10,000 of them filling the arena around the first fairway and the 17th and 18th greens and giving the home stretch an even bigger buzz, certainly got value for their £10 entry fee, not forgetting the high proportion of under-16s who were admitted free for a day they will remember longest of all. As Jordan Spieth, who provided the added dimension of a player only narrowly missing out on a third successive Major that would have kept his Grand Slam ambitions alive, said: "That's a hell of a Major."

What happened, simply put, is this. Johnson

*Marc Leishman hits the first of the 66 strokes that would put him in a play-off.*

scored a 66, as it turned out the lowest score by a Champion in the final round on the Old Course by three strokes. But so did Marc Leishman, and when the 2010 winner Oosthuizen managed to do what Spieth and Jason Day could not and birdie the 18th, there was a three-way play-off over the first, second, 17th and 18th holes. Oosthuizen birdied the first; Johnson birdied the first two and won by a stroke from the South African, with Leishman two further back.

As for how it happened, as Johnson said to open his excellent winner's speech in front of the Royal and Ancient Clubhouse, "This could take awhile." Here goes with the edited highlights.

First, a disclaimer. Zach Johnson, the Champion Golfer of the Year, is in no way related to Dustin Johnson, leader of this Open for the first two days — not familiarly, nor in their golfing styles. While Dustin has the big-hitting game that could win the Masters or any Major and that overpowered the Old Course on Thursday, Zach did win a Green Jacket by famously laying-up at every par 5 at Augusta National in 2007, and his quality in the pitching and putting departments has now brought him two Major titles. The 39-year-old, who

*Padraig Harrington briefly tied the lead before falling back*

*Anthony Wall enjoyed his run to a tie for 12th place.*

grew up in Cedar Rapids, Iowa, and now resides in Sea Island, Georgia, became the 14th player to do the Masters-Open double and the sixth to sing the Augusta-St Andrews duet.

Three late bogeys in his third round meant Dustin Johnson was teeing off in the middle of the pack on Monday and a second successive 75 only sent him further down the leaderboard. Zach Johnson was headed in the opposite direction. Though he felt rested after not hitting a ball on Saturday, having completed his second round the previous day, Johnson did not score well in the third round until he posted two birdies in the last three holes. It was something to bring into the final day.

He teed-off alongside England's Danny Willett an hour before the final pairing of Oosthuizen and Paul Dunne, the young amateur who shared the 54-hole lead with the South African and Day, who

*Thumbs up: Oliver Schniederjans' last day as an amateur.*

*Sergio Garcia's charge ended when his putter went cold.*

was in the penultimate pairing with Spieth. Johnson had a simple plan. "I clearly had to be somewhat aggressive early on because those outward holes are the ones you've got to take advantage of," he said. "I felt if I could get a bit of momentum early on, then who knows what could happen?"

There were some low scores out there and Johnson promptly matched the best outward nine of the day with 31 strokes to the turn. He holed from 18 feet for a 3 at the second, from 35 feet from the fringe on the fourth, two-putted for a 4 at the fifth, hit a wedge from 99 yards to three feet at the seventh and hit another short wedge shot to six feet at the ninth.

Why stop there? He two-putted from 95 feet for a 3 at the 10th and holed from eight feet for his seventh birdie of the day at the 12th. When he had holed that short putt at the seventh, Johnson was sharing the lead. By the time he made the birdie at the 10th, he was ahead on his own.

---

*Danny Willett, who finished in a tie for sixth, had the honour of playing the final round with Zach Johnson.*

*Leishman took the lead with this putt on the 12th green.*

There were periods when players needed to make birdies just to hold their positions on the leaderboard. Bogeys were injurious in the extreme. Dunne had two at the first two holes, after leaving his second at the first short of the burn and driving onto the 18th green of the New Course off the second tee.

Had the chance to become the first amateur winner for 85 years overwhelmed the 22-year-old Irishman? He said not, it was just that he had not settled in the squally showers that swept across the course. He actually birdied two of the next three holes, but it all drifted away on the back nine. A 78 dropped him out of contention not just for the Claret Jug but for the Silver Medal, which, after a mighty contest, went to Jordan Niebrugge, of the United States, for finishing in a share of sixth place.

Oosthuizen did birdie the first and he needed

# Louis almost swings it again at the Home of Golf

To watch Louis Oosthuizen in full flow is to witness poetry in motion. By common consent the South African has one of the best, most well-oiled swings in the game — one that is like the man himself; it looks humble, but packs a surprising punch.

It is a swing that carried Oosthuizen to an emphatic victory in The Open in 2010 and almost did so again in 2015. With one victory already under his belt on the Old Course, the former Champion went into the three-man play-off for the Claret Jug as a narrow favourite over Zach Johnson and Marc Leishman.

He had the momentum with him, having birdied the final hole in regulation play to draw level at

the top of the leaderboard on 273, 15 under par, but he was taking nothing for granted. He had tasted

defeat to Bubba Watson in a play-off for the 2012 Masters and was

only too aware that over four holes anything could happen.

In the event he came up one stroke short of Johnson and was left disappointed once again. He birdied the first extra hole, but the putts at the next three just would not drop. He matched Rickie Fowler from 2014 in finishing as a runner-up at both the US Open and The Open.

"It's never nice to lose a play-off, but I'll take a lot out of this week," Oosthuizen said. "I was really motivated to win this week. I love this place and can't wait for it to come back here again."

—*Peter Dixon*

*Dream over, Paul Dunne at the 18th.*

# Jordan earns Amateur honours

It is a harsh school when you can be leading The Open after 54 holes and not end up with the Silver Medal. Teeing off in the last pairing, Paul Dunne slipped out of contention for the Claret Jug with a 78, and such was the competition among the amateurs that he was overtaken in that race, too.

Instead the honours went to American Jordan Niebrugge, who was also in the thick of the main action. He finished with a 70 to match his playing partner, Sergio Garcia, and join the Spaniard, Justin Rose and Danny Willett in sixth place. It was the best finish in The Open by an amateur since Chris Wood's fifth place in 2008. "It's definitely a dream come true," said the 21-year-old. "This means the world to me. It was amazing walking down the 18th with Sergio, it's just an awesome amphitheatre with all those people."

While Niebrugge intended to complete his final year at Oklahoma State University, compatriot Oliver Schniederjans announced he would be turning professional at the Canadian Open the following week after going out in 31 for a 67 to tie for 12th place. "It was an amazing final day as an amateur, I couldn't ask for anything more special," he said.

Shropshire's Ashley Chesters, who had a putt for an eagle at the 10th to tie for the lead, suffered a late double-bogey at the 15th and also tied for 12th on nine under par. All three broke the previous record 72-hole score by an amateur of 281 by Iain Pyman in 1993 and Tiger Woods in 1996.

—*Andy Farrell*

*Adam Scott had problems on the last five holes.*

to, since Spieth, who started one behind the trio of leaders, had too, while Harrington birdied the first two. The two-time Champion also birdied the fifth to tie for the lead but then attempted to drive close to the sixth green and lost a ball in the bushes. "Things were going well, why not take it on?" he reasoned. A double-bogey there and a three-putt bogey at the eighth spelled the end of another Irishman's challenge.

Then came what is becoming an annual tradition at The Open: the Adam Scott charge. The Australian matched Johnson's outward 31 and collected his fifth birdie in six holes at the 10th. Now he was tied for the lead with Johnson at 15 under par. At Muirfield in 2013, Scott had a similar surge before dropping back, while at Royal Lytham & St Annes the year before he led by four with four to play but bogeyed them all to lose to Ernie Els.

His determination to claim a Claret Jug may one

*Johnson and caddie Damon Green celebrate Zach's putt at the last.*

## Round of the Day: **Zach Johnson – 66**

OFFICIAL SCORECARD
THE 144TH OPEN
ST ANDREWS

Zach JOHNSON
Game 34
Monday 20 July at 1:30pm

|  | FOR R&A USE ONLY | ROUND 4 |
|---|---|---|
| 54 HOLE TOTAL | 207 | 72 HOLE TOTAL |
| THIS ROUND | 66 | 273 |
| 72 HOLE TOTAL | 273 | |

ROUND 4     VERIFIED

| Hole | 1 | 2 | 3 | 4 | 5 | 6 | 7 | 8 | 9 | Out |
|---|---|---|---|---|---|---|---|---|---|---|
| Yards | 375 | 452 | 398 | 480 | 570 | 414 | 371 | 174 | 352 | 3586 |
| Par | 4 | 4 | 4 | 4 | 5 | 4 | 4 | 3 | 4 | 36 |
| Score | 4 | 3 | 4 | 3 | 4 | 4 | 3 | 3 | 3 | 31 |

| Hole | 10 | 11 | 12 | 13 | 14 | 15 | 16 | 17 | 18 | In | Total |
|---|---|---|---|---|---|---|---|---|---|---|---|
| Yards | 386 | 174 | 348 | 465 | 614 | 455 | 418 | 495 | 356 | 3711 | 7297 |
| Par | 4 | 3 | 4 | 4 | 5 | 4 | 4 | 4 | 4 | 36 | 72 |
| Score | 3 | 3 | 3 | 5 | 5 | 4 | 4 | 5 | 3 | 35 | 66 |

Signature of Marker

Signature of Competitor
Zach Johnson

day be rewarded but not this year. He dropped five strokes in the last five holes, including a double-bogey at the last. He had started leaking oil when he failed to get up-and-down from a bunker at the 14th, but he stalled completely when he missed a tap-in from a foot with his broom-handled putter at the next. "I don't really have an explanation," Scott admitted. "I went to tap it in and it lipped out. Just one of those stupid things that happens. I just didn't execute over the last five holes."

Johnson did, but not without blemishes on the scorecard. He found a bunker at the 13th and took 5, as he did at the 17th after hitting his second shot fat with a 3-wood and leaving it 100 yards short of the

*Jason Day covers his eyes after missing his birdie putt to make the play-off.*

green. He now briefly fell two behind Leishman, but at the last he rolled in a 28-footer with an accompanying punch of the air and a celebratory jig from his caddie, Damon Green.

"The emotion was because it was the 72nd and I knew I had a good round going," said Johnson after posting 15 under par as the clubhouse target. "But it was brief because I knew I had to get my emotions in check to get ready for what happened." Translation: He wasn't sure it was good enough to win, but it might get him into a play-off.

That was wise, because when Leishman bogeyed the 16th hole moments later, he dropped back to 15 under par. It had been another superb round from the 31-year-old Australian, who carded the best-of-the-week 64 in the third round. Apparently winters in Warrnambool, Victoria, are similar to summers in St Andrews, Fife; he felt at home.

Four birdies in the first five holes put him in a

tie for the lead, but it was not until three birdies later, when he holed a three-footer at the 12th, that Leishman took the lead on his own. He holed a good par-save at the 15th but drifted into a bunker at the next. He came out to four feet but missed the putt. "I didn't putt a bad putt, it just didn't do what I thought it was going to do," he explained. "I hit a really good bunker shot and didn't finish it off, but I'm not going to look back and be sour about anything."

He got his par at the 17th and then had a chance at the last to pip Johnson. "I just misread the putt," he said. "Hit it good, it didn't break." Like Johnson, his 66 left him at 15 under par.

Four players remained out on the course and the three professionals all had a chance. That meant Spieth could still join Ben Hogan as winner of the Masters, the US Open and The Open in the same year but, as throughout the week, that had not

*Grand Slam over: Jordan Spieth pulled his drive at the last and found the Valley of Sin with his second shot.*

always looked the case. His second birdie of the day, at the fifth, tied him briefly for the lead, but by the time he had a 3 at the next he was one behind. He dropped further back with a double-bogey at the short eighth after inexplicably racing his first putt off the green.

"There was absolutely no reason to hit that putt off the green," admitted the 21-year-old Texan. "But I'd left so many putts short throughout the week that I said I wasn't leaving this one short. Instead I hit it off the other side of the green where it was really dead."

Spieth had bounced back from all the three-putts during the week, surely a four-putt had done for him? Yet birdies at the next two holes kept him in touch. And somehow, or rather in yet another

*Earlier Spieth tied for the lead at the 16th.*

*Leishman plays his approach at the second extra hole.*

example of how he can seize the moment when it really matters, he rolled in a 50-footer at the 16th and was now tied for the lead.

History was within his grasp if he could get home in seven strokes, or at least eight for a play-off. He was not thinking about history. "None of that came into my head because 17 is so brutal and 18 is tough to get close. It was how can we work our butts off to make a 4 on 17 and give ourselves a putt to win."

Spieth needed to hole a six-footer on the 17th for his 4, but for once his magical putting touch deserted him. Then at the 18th his drive finished so far left, by the grandstand, that his approach almost inevitably came up short in the Valley of Sin. "Who would have thought a drive on 18 was going to be what really hurt me at the end," he said. "It's hard not to hit a good one on that hole."

Needing a 3 to tie, there was no Rocca miracle.

*Not close enough, Oosthuizen rues his second at the 17th.*

*Leishman needed to hole his second at the last to have any chance, but disappointment came with new-found perspective.*

His putt ran up the slope but was always just left of the hole. "It was a good putt with the right speed, (but) it was hard to get it on line. I knew it was not going to break back to the right." A 69 left him one short, on 14 under par. Just as Arnold Palmer was one short in 1960 and Jack Nicklaus in 1972. "I made a lot of the right decisions down the stretch and have certainly closed out plenty of tournaments, this just wasn't one of them," Spieth said. "I'm not going to beat myself up too bad."

Alongside Spieth, Day had been steady again, going bogey-free for the third time in the week. While everyone else was collecting birdies for fun, Day only found a pair, at the fifth and sixth, but all the pars had not hurt him. Suddenly, on the final green, he had a far better chance than Spieth of getting a birdie to join the play-off. It was from just over 20 feet, left-to-right, and the Aussie left it tantalisingly just short of the hole.

"All I wanted was to put a good stroke on it," said Day, head in his hands. "I didn't want to blast it through the break. Unfortunately, I thought it was a little faster, and it just pulled up." It was the 27-year-old's best finish in The Open and his sixth top-four in all Majors. "It was frustrating how it finished," he said. "I've been working very hard to accomplish my first Major. I really want to have that shot at immortality. It'll come soon." Indeed it did, at the PGA Championship a month later.

Finally, there was Oosthuizen, marching up the 18th in very different circumstances to his runaway victory in 2010. There had been four three-putts but only two bogeys, and even though, as he said, "St Andrews showed its teeth" on the way in, he holed brave par-savers at the 16th and 17th holes and then a vital five-footer for birdie at the last. A 69 and he, too, was in at 15 under par.

While announcer Ivor Robson returned to the

*Johnson chips over the green at the 17th in the play-off but got down in two for a bogey.*

## Not quite job Dunne for retiring Robson

"On the tee, from Ireland, Paul Dunne."

So said Ivor Robson, in his familiar lilt, concise and precise as ever, as he ended his career as the first tee announcer at The Open. Dunne was the 18,995th and last player the 74-year-old from Moffat had introduced — at least until the play-off when he did the honours three more times, a fitting encore.

Robson, a former club professional, took on the role at Carnoustie in 1975, going on to become the official starter of the European Tour. On Tuesday evening he was a special guest at the past Champions' dinner, while on Friday fellow retiree Tom Watson made his own presentation of a signed flag.

"Ivor started his announcing at the 1975 Open Championship, which was my first Open too," said Watson. "So we came in together and we are going out together. He is iconic and he has been a big part of The Open Championship."

Robson said: "I've had a wonderful time with all the players. They are a credit to the game, they really are.

"It's been a great honour. The Open has been a massive part of my life, but there is no one bigger than the game. I'm part of a team and we all help to keep the event running smoothly. Yes, it's my last, but The Open goes on and it will continue to be run well.

"St Andrews is a perfect place for me to bow out."

—*Andy Farrell*

*Almost there: Johnson's approach at the fourth extra hole safely finds the green.*

*Missed putts by Oosthuizen for par at the 17th...*

*Johnson salutes the gallery in victory.*

first tee one last time before his retirement for the play-off, the thought that Oosthuizen held the momentum was confirmed when the South African followed Johnson in for a birdie at the first. But his chance at the next just missed, while Johnson made another 15-footer to take the lead.

Leishman had found a divot off the tee on the first and made a 5. "I was on the back foot after that," he said. He also bogeyed the 17th, but all three did. "I gave it my best shot, but Zach played well in the play-off," said the Australian, whose wife had been seriously ill earlier in the year. "It's disappointing, but I'm happy I've just finished second in The Open. I can go home and hug Audrey and the kids and celebrate a little, maybe not with the Claret Jug to drink out of but I'll find something else."

Johnson had a scare when he pitched over the 17th green but he still made his 5, while Oosthuizen three-putted from long range. At the last again, Johnson could not make another 3 but nor could

*...and birdie on the 18th dashed his hopes of a second Open.*

Oosthuizen, who missed his 10-footer on the left lip of the hole. "He left the door open on 17 but I could not take advantage. I hit great putts to make the play-off but misread 17 and 18 in the play-off," said Oosthuizen, who lost in extra time to Bubba Watson at the 2012 Masters. "It is never nice to lose a play-off. I was really motivated to win this Championship. I love this place. I've said it a thousand times. I can't wait to come back here again."

Patience and perseverance were the keys to success according to the new Champion Golfer of the Year, who admitted that either of the other two men in the play-off could have easily claimed the Claret Jug. Of the ending, Johnson said: "You never want to see a championship, specifically The Open, end on a miss. I don't particularly care to see that as a spectator, but fortunately I made a few putts prior to that and that put me in this position, so I feel blessed."

Among the first to congratulate Johnson after his caddie and wife, Kim, was Spieth, who had hung around to watch the play-off. Johnson said, "He's a good friend of mine and he's a phenomenal talent, but he is a better person than he is a golfer. I can't describe the magnitude as to what he was going through because I've never been in that position."

Johnson also struggled to put into words what his victory meant, coming at what he said was his "most fun golf tournament." Of the Claret Jug, he said: "I'm humbled right now because of what's in my lap and the names that are etched on this piece of metal that is very special. It's a dream realised. I am a little bit in shock."

After such a tumultuous day, we all were. Yet a man with an inner calmness had prevailed. With a rare presence of mind in his moment of triumph, Johnson added: "This is not my legacy. I realise it is only a game. Granted, as a professional athlete and as a golfer, I'm going to relish this. I'm humbled by this. But my legacy should be my kids, my family, that kind of thing."

*Johnson receives a victory kiss from his wife Kim…*

*…while Spieth was quick to congratulate the new Champion.*

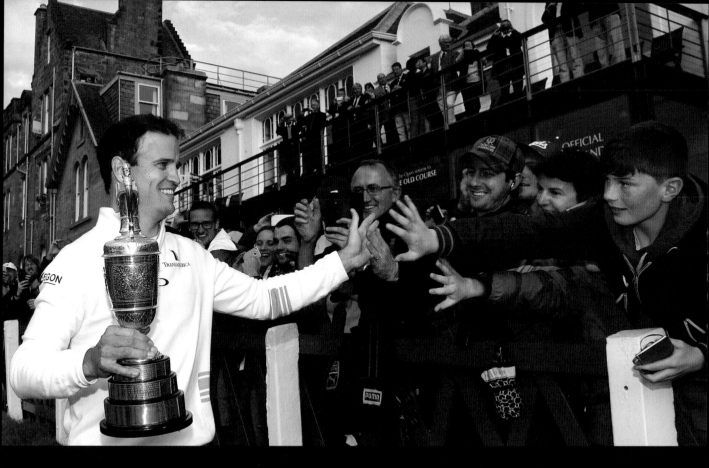

## It's a
## FACT

Zach Johnson posted the lowest final round by a Champion at St Andrews, beating the 69s of Jack Nicklaus (1978), Seve Ballesteros (1984) and Tiger Woods (2000), but not before winning the sixth play-off in St Andrews Opens. Neither Louis Oosthuizen nor Marc Leishman emulated Davie Strath in refusing to play-off in 1876.

## CHAMPIONSHIP HOLE SUMMARY

| HOLE | PAR | YARDS | EAGLES | BIRDIES | PARS | BOGEYS | D.BOGEYS | OTHER | RANK | AVERAGE |
|------|-----|-------|--------|---------|------|--------|----------|-------|------|---------|
| 1 | 4 | 375 | 0 | 120 | 310 | 38 | 4 | 0 | 13 | 3.843 |
| 2 | 4 | 452 | 0 | 73 | 316 | 74 | 8 | 1 | 8 | 4.042 |
| 3 | 4 | 398 | 0 | 107 | 325 | 38 | 2 | 0 | 11 | 3.862 |
| 4 | 4 | 480 | 0 | 49 | 312 | 103 | 7 | 1 | 4 | 4.150 |
| 5 | 5 | 570 | 10 | 257 | 182 | 22 | 1 | 0 | 18 | 4.464 |
| 6 | 4 | 414 | 1 | 118 | 304 | 45 | 4 | 0 | 12 | 3.858 |
| 7 | 4 | 371 | 0 | 121 | 325 | 26 | 0 | 0 | 15 | 3.799 |
| 8 | 3 | 174 | 0 | 44 | 371 | 49 | 8 | 0 | 7 | 3.044 |
| 9 | 4 | 352 | 0 | 122 | 322 | 25 | 3 | 0 | 14 | 3.807 |
| OUT | 36 | 3,586 | 11 | 1,011 | 2,767 | 420 | 37 | 2 | | 34.871 |
| 10 | 4 | 386 | 3 | 148 | 277 | 40 | 3 | 1 | 16 | 3.778 |
| 11 | 3 | 174 | 1 | 73 | 287 | 105 | 6 | 0 | 6 | 3.089 |
| 12 | 4 | 348 | 0 | 79 | 316 | 71 | 5 | 1 | 9 | 4.011 |
| 13 | 4 | 465 | 0 | 51 | 293 | 117 | 9 | 2 | 3 | 4.191 |
| 14 | 5 | 614 | 3 | 106 | 266 | 80 | 15 | 2 | 10 | 5.008 |
| 15 | 4 | 455 | 0 | 45 | 336 | 85 | 5 | 1 | 5 | 4.112 |
| 16 | 4 | 418 | 0 | 25 | 334 | 92 | 16 | 5 | 2 | 4.242 |
| 17 | 4 | 495 | 0 | 9 | 203 | 217 | 32 | 11 | 1 | 4.655 |
| 18 | 4 | 356 | 1 | 149 | 287 | 33 | 2 | 0 | 17 | 3.758 |
| IN | 36 | 3,711 | 8 | 685 | 2,599 | 840 | 93 | 23 | | 36.843 |
| TOTAL | 72 | 7,297 | 19 | 1,696 | 5,366 | 1,260 | 130 | 25 | | 71.414 |

# FOURTH ROUND LEADERS

| HOLE | 1 | 2 | 3 | 4 | 5 | 6 | 7 | 8 | 9 | 10 | 11 | 12 | 13 | 14 | 15 | 16 | 17 | 18 | TOTAL |
|------|---|---|---|---|---|---|---|---|---|----|----|----|----|----|----|----|----|----|-------|
| PAR | 4 | 4 | 4 | 4 | 5 | 4 | 4 | 3 | 4 | 4 | 3 | 4 | 4 | 5 | 4 | 4 | 4 | 4 | |
| Zach Johnson | 4 | 3 | 4 | 3 | 4 | 4 | 3 | 3 | 3 | 3 | 3 | 3 | 5 | 5 | 4 | 4 | 5 | 3 | 66-273 |
| Marc Leishman | 3 | 4 | 3 | 3 | 4 | 4 | 4 | 3 | 3 | 3 | 3 | 3 | 4 | 5 | 4 | 5 | 4 | 4 | 66-273 |
| Louis Oosthuizen | 3 | 4 | 4 | 4 | 5 | 3 | 4 | 4 | 3 | 4 | 3 | 3 | 5 | 5 | 4 | 4 | 4 | 3 | 69-273 |
| Jordan Spieth | 3 | 4 | 4 | 4 | 4 | 3 | 4 | 5 | 3 | 3 | 3 | 4 | 4 | 5 | 4 | 3 | 5 | 4 | 69-274 |
| Jason Day | 4 | 4 | 4 | 4 | 3 | 4 | 3 | 4 | 3 | 4 | 4 | 4 | 5 | 4 | 4 | 4 | 4 | 4 | 70-274 |
| Danny Willett | 3 | 4 | 4 | 5 | 5 | 4 | 4 | 4 | 4 | 4 | 2 | 3 | 3 | 4 | 4 | 4 | 5 | 4 | 70-277 |
| Justin Rose | 4 | 4 | 4 | 4 | 4 | 4 | 4 | 3 | 4 | 4 | 3 | 3 | 5 | 5 | 4 | 4 | 4 | 3 | 70-277 |
| Sergio Garcia | 3 | 4 | 3 | 4 | 4 | 4 | 3 | 3 | 4 | 3 | 5 | 5 | 5 | 5 | 4 | 5 | 4 | 4 | 70-277 |
| Jordan Niebrugge* | 4 | 4 | 4 | 3 | 4 | 3 | 4 | 3 | 4 | 4 | 3 | 4 | 4 | 4 | 5 | 4 | 5 | 4 | 70-277 |

■ EAGLE OR BETTER  ■ BIRDIES  ■ BOGEYS  ■ DBL BOGEYS/WORSE

## SCORING SUMMARY

### FOURTH ROUND SCORES

| | |
|---|---|
| Players Under Par | 40 |
| Players At Par | 11 |
| Players Over Par | 29 |

### CHAMPIONSHIP SCORES

| | |
|---|---|
| Rounds Under Par | 225 |
| Rounds At Par | 65 |
| Rounds Over Par | 182 |

### LOW SCORES

**Low First Nine**

| | |
|---|---|
| Zach Johnson | 31 |
| Marc Leishman | 31 |
| Adam Scott | 31 |
| Oliver Schniederjans* | 31 |
| Branden Grace | 31 |
| Jamie Donaldson | 31 |

**Low Second Nine**

| | |
|---|---|
| Danny Willett | 33 |
| Brendon Todd | 33 |
| Billy Horschel | 33 |

**Low Round**

| | |
|---|---|
| Zach Johnson | 66 |
| Marc Leishman | 66 |
| Brendon Todd | 66 |
| Scott Arnold | 66 |

## FOURTH ROUND HOLE SUMMARY

| HOLE | PAR | YARDS | EAGLES | BIRDIES | PARS | BOGEYS | D.BOGEYS | OTHER | RANK | AVERAGE |
|------|-----|-------|--------|---------|------|--------|----------|-------|------|---------|
| 1 | 4 | 375 | 0 | 28 | 44 | 8 | 0 | 0 | 15 | 3.750 |
| 2 | 4 | 452 | 0 | 17 | 51 | 11 | 1 | 0 | 10 | 3.950 |
| 3 | 4 | 398 | 0 | 12 | 59 | 9 | 0 | 0 | 8 | 3.962 |
| 4 | 4 | 480 | 0 | 13 | 51 | 15 | 1 | 0 | 7 | 4.050 |
| 5 | 5 | 570 | 2 | 52 | 25 | 0 | 1 | 0 | 18 | 4.325 |
| 6 | 4 | 414 | 0 | 24 | 50 | 5 | 1 | 0 | 13 | 3.788 |
| 7 | 4 | 371 | 0 | 22 | 55 | 3 | 0 | 0 | 14 | 3.762 |
| 8 | 3 | 174 | 0 | 3 | 64 | 11 | 2 | 0 | 6 | 3.150 |
| 9 | 4 | 352 | 0 | 28 | 51 | 1 | 0 | 0 | 16 | 3.662 |
| OUT | 36 | 3,586 | 2 | 199 | 450 | 63 | 6 | 0 | | 34.400 |
| 10 | 4 | 386 | 0 | 43 | 35 | 2 | 0 | 0 | 17 | 3.488 |
| 11 | 3 | 174 | 0 | 10 | 66 | 4 | 0 | 0 | 11 | 2.925 |
| 12 | 4 | 348 | 0 | 16 | 51 | 13 | 0 | 0 | 8 | 3.962 |
| 13 | 4 | 465 | 0 | 5 | 46 | 27 | 2 | 0 | 2 | 4.325 |
| 14 | 5 | 614 | 0 | 6 | 54 | 16 | 4 | 0 | 4 | 5.225 |
| 15 | 4 | 455 | 0 | 3 | 60 | 16 | 1 | 0 | 5 | 4.188 |
| 16 | 4 | 418 | 0 | 3 | 55 | 21 | 1 | 0 | 3 | 4.250 |
| 17 | 4 | 495 | 0 | 1 | 26 | 43 | 8 | 2 | 1 | 4.800 |
| 18 | 4 | 356 | 1 | 18 | 52 | 8 | 1 | 0 | 12 | 3.875 |
| IN | 36 | 3,711 | 1 | 105 | 445 | 150 | 17 | 2 | | 37.038 |
| TOTAL | 72 | 7,297 | 3 | 304 | 895 | 213 | 23 | 2 | | 71.438 |

> *Jordan congratulated me, he's a good friend. He's a phenomenal talent but he's a better person than he is a golfer. I can't begin to describe the magnitude of what he was trying to do.*
>
> —Zach Johnson

> *I love this tournament. I love these crowds. I love these courses. I'm just going to keep giving myself chances until things happen — and then hopefully I'll manage to win at least one of these.*
>
> —Sergio Garcia

> *Second at a Major. You know, it's not first, but I'll take it.*
>
> —Louis Oosthuizen

> *The conditions didn't suit me, but that's not an excuse. I should just get used to the conditions more. It was just a day that my golf wasn't there.*
>
> —Paul Dunne

> *It was good to play with Zach today. You can actually look back and see how they won it, what they didn't do, stuff you can learn from.*
>
> —Danny Willett

> *My speed control was really what cost me this week, the five three-putts the second round, then just my speed control in general wasn't great.*
>
> —Jordan Spieth

> *I really want to have that shot at immortality. It'll soon come my way. I've just got to be patient with it.*
>
> —Jason Day

> *I'll probably cut the grass tomorrow. I do love cutting grass.*
>
> —Anthony Wall

# The Champion Golfer of the Year from Cedar Rapids, Iowa

*John Hopkins on the "normal guy" who claimed Golf's Greatest Prize.*

You might not have noticed but there are Johnsons at most golf clubs. There's the Dustin, who is tall, long-limbed and powerful and, be honest, you want to hit the ball like him. Languid swing, firm and strong through the ball and whoosh! Away it goes. Then there's the Zach who is small, tidy, quietly spoken and understated, a golfer you know about but don't give much regard to.

Truth is, you'd be better off copying the Zach type than dreaming you can hit it like the Dustin. The Zach type wears glasses, doesn't weigh very much, or hit it very far, and when you play a match or a medal against him you fancy your chances. Yet he beats you on the 14th green or by six or seven strokes and you are left wondering: what happened?

It happened at St Andrews in Zach Johnson style. He didn't wrestle the course to the ground and stamp on it. He didn't drive any of the par 4s. Not many at any rate. That's not within his compass.

Rather he stole up on the Old Course, plotting every move with care and executing his shots with skill and thought. From 100 yards in, he was deadly with his shots to the green and then deadly with his putter. Only one player had fewer putts in the 72 holes than Johnson. He birdied the 72nd hole to set a target and then birdied the first two holes of the play-off as well.

We had gone to St Andrews expecting a mugging of the Old Course by players who could drive three of the par 4s and reach both par 5s in two. We came away admitting that there had been a mugging but it was done by Zach in his quiet, understated way.

When he plays golf as well as he did at St Andrews, it is no surprise to learn that prior to this Open, he had won 11 events on the PGA Tour in the US in the past decade, including the 2007 Masters. Only three others had done this — Tiger Woods, Phil Mickelson and Rory McIlroy. Notice anything about these three? They are all big hitters. Johnson is not.

In the success Johnson, 39, has made for himself he is reminiscent of Larry Nelson, who was christened "my baby-faced chicken killer" by Dave Marr, his captain, at the 1981 Ryder Cup for the way he won his four matches at Walton Heath, just as he had won his five matches two years earlier at The Greenbrier.

"For him to pull that off was just like David and Goliath," said Damon Green, Johnson's caddie at St Andrews. "He's my little bulldog. He gets on your pants leg and won't give up until he gets some flesh. My man's got the biggest heart out there."

The thing about Johnson is that although he deserves respect, he acts and talks as though he does not. It's not an act either. "I'm just a normal guy from Cedar Rapids, Iowa," he kept saying after he had won the Masters.

Same again after winning The Open. "I'm just a guy from Iowa who has been blessed with a talent and this game provides great opportunity. God gave me the ability to play a game and I try to take it seriously."

There, he said it. The God word. Johnson is a believer. As he went about his business on the Old

Course, he often had his nose in his yardage book.

Johnson was looking at words from the Bible. Psalm 27, verse 14:

*Be patient, wait for the Lord,*
*Be courageous and brave.*
*Yes, be patient, wait for the Lord.*

Reading these words, as he did so often, helped him focus. "Gets me down to my priorities," he said.

Hindsight suggests that we ought to have known Zach Johnson would be at home on his third visit to the Old Course for an Open, even though he had missed the cut in 2005 and finished tied 76th in 2010. The course is 7,200 yards long, which is a few hundred yards shorter and more in Johnson's wheelhouse than some.

Go at the Old Course like a bull at a gate and you will find yourself in one of its many bunkers, or on the incorrect fairway, or on the wrong side of, say, the fifth and 13th green, which is one of the biggest in the world. Allow yourself to get worked up by these idiosyncrasies and you're out of the game. Embrace them, as Johnson did, and you will do well. Woo the course, don't overpower it. That's the secret.

Johnson is a decent man, a hard worker who is better at 39 than he was at 31, when he won the Masters. The older he has got the more he has come to love golf. "I've enjoyed practising more, I've enjoyed working out more. I think quality hard work creates luck," he said.

He proved that all right at St Andrews.

# The 144ᵀᴴ Open

# Complete Scores

| HOLE | | | 1 | 2 | 3 | 4 | 5 | 6 | 7 | 8 | 9 | 10 | 11 | 12 | 13 | 14 | 15 | 16 | 17 | 18 | |
|---|---|---|---|---|---|---|---|---|---|---|---|---|---|---|---|---|---|---|---|---|---|
| PAR | POSITION | | 4 | 4 | 4 | 4 | 5 | 4 | 3 | 4 | 4 | 3 | 4 | 4 | 5 | 4 | 4 | 4 | 4 | 4 | TOTAL |
| **Zach Johnson** | T2 | Round 1 | 3 | 3 | 4 | 4 | 4 | 3 | 4 | 3 | 3 | 3 | 3 | 4 | 4 | 5 | 4 | 4 | 5 | 3 | 66 |
| USA | T4 | Round 2 | 4 | 4 | 4 | 4 | 4 | 3 | 4 | 3 | 4 | 4 | 4 | 5 | 3 | 5 | 5 | 4 | 4 | 3 | 71 |
| £1,150,000 | T6 | Round 3 | 4 | 4 | 4 | 4 | 5 | 4 | 4 | 3 | 4 | 4 | 3 | 4 | 4 | 4 | 4 | 3 | 5 | 3 | 70 |
| | | Round 4 | 4 | 3 | 4 | 3 | 4 | 4 | 3 | 3 | 3 | 3 | 3 | 3 | 5 | 5 | 4 | 4 | 5 | 3 | 66-**273** |
| | 1 | Play-off | 3 | 3 | | | | | | | | | | | | | | | 5 | 4 | **15** |
| **Marc Leishman** | T24 | Round 1 | 3 | 4 | 3 | 4 | 5 | 4 | 4 | 3 | 4 | 3 | 3 | 4 | 5 | 5 | 5 | 4 | 4 | 3 | 70 |
| Australia | T50 | Round 2 | 4 | 4 | 4 | 4 | 5 | 4 | 4 | 3 | 6 | 4 | 2 | 4 | 4 | 5 | 4 | 4 | 5 | 3 | 73 |
| £536,500 | T6 | Round 3 | 4 | 4 | 4 | 3 | 4 | 4 | 3 | 2 | 4 | 3 | 2 | 4 | 3 | 5 | 3 | 4 | 4 | 4 | 64 |
| | | Round 4 | 3 | 4 | 3 | 3 | 4 | 4 | 4 | 3 | 3 | 3 | 3 | 3 | 4 | 5 | 4 | 5 | 4 | 4 | 66-**273** |
| | T2 | Play-off | 5 | 4 | | | | | | | | | | | | | | | 5 | 4 | **18** |
| **Louis Oosthuizen** | T8 | Round 1 | 4 | 4 | 4 | 4 | 4 | 4 | 3 | 3 | 3 | 4 | 2 | 4 | 5 | 4 | 4 | 4 | 4 | 3 | 67 |
| South Africa | T4 | Round 2 | 4 | 4 | 4 | 5 | 4 | 4 | 3 | 3 | 3 | 4 | 3 | 4 | 4 | 6 | 3 | 4 | 4 | 4 | 70 |
| £536,500 | T1 | Round 3 | 4 | 4 | 4 | 3 | 4 | 4 | 3 | 4 | 4 | 4 | 2 | 5 | 4 | 4 | 3 | 4 | 4 | 3 | 67 |
| | | Round 4 | 3 | 4 | 4 | 4 | 5 | 3 | 4 | 4 | 3 | 4 | 3 | 3 | 5 | 5 | 4 | 4 | 4 | 3 | 69-**273** |
| | T2 | Play-off | 3 | 4 | | | | | | | | | | | | | | | 5 | 4 | **16** |
| **Jordan Spieth** | T8 | Round 1 | 3 | 3 | 4 | 4 | 4 | 3 | 3 | 4 | 4 | 4 | 2 | 4 | 5 | 5 | 4 | 4 | 5 | 3 | 67 |
| USA | T14 | Round 2 | 4 | 4 | 4 | 4 | 6 | 3 | 3 | 4 | 3 | 4 | 4 | 4 | 4 | 5 | 4 | 4 | 5 | 3 | 72 |
| £295,000 | 4 | Round 3 | 3 | 4 | 4 | 4 | 4 | 4 | 3 | 3 | 5 | 3 | 2 | 3 | 4 | 5 | 3 | 4 | 4 | 4 | 66 |
| | T4 | Round 4 | 3 | 4 | 4 | 4 | 4 | 3 | 4 | 5 | 3 | 3 | 3 | 4 | 4 | 5 | 4 | 3 | 5 | 4 | 69-**274** |
| **Jason Day** | T2 | Round 1 | 4 | 3 | 4 | 4 | 4 | 3 | 4 | 3 | 4 | 3 | 3 | 4 | 4 | 4 | 3 | 4 | 4 | 4 | 66 |
| Australia | T4 | Round 2 | 3 | 5 | 4 | 4 | 5 | 4 | 3 | 3 | 3 | 4 | 3 | 5 | 5 | 5 | 4 | 4 | 4 | 3 | 71 |
| £295,000 | T1 | Round 3 | 4 | 4 | 4 | 4 | 4 | 3 | 4 | 3 | 4 | 4 | 2 | 4 | 3 | 5 | 3 | 4 | 4 | 4 | 67 |
| | T4 | Round 4 | 4 | 4 | 4 | 4 | 4 | 3 | 4 | 3 | 4 | 4 | 3 | 4 | 4 | 5 | 4 | 4 | 4 | 4 | 70-**274** |
| **Danny Willett** | T2 | Round 1 | 3 | 3 | 3 | 4 | 5 | 4 | 4 | 3 | 4 | 2 | 4 | 3 | 5 | 4 | 4 | 4 | 4 | 3 | 66 |
| England | 2 | Round 2 | 4 | 3 | 4 | 4 | 4 | 4 | 4 | 3 | 3 | 3 | 3 | 4 | 4 | 5 | 5 | 4 | 5 | 3 | 69 |
| £196,000 | T6 | Round 3 | 4 | 4 | 4 | 4 | 4 | 4 | 4 | 3 | 3 | 3 | 3 | 4 | 5 | 6 | 4 | 4 | 5 | 4 | 72 |
| | T6 | Round 4 | 3 | 4 | 4 | 5 | 5 | 4 | 4 | 4 | 4 | 4 | 2 | 3 | 3 | 4 | 4 | 4 | 5 | 4 | 70-**277** |
| **Justin Rose** | T41 | Round 1 | 3 | 4 | 4 | 3 | 4 | 4 | 3 | 3 | 4 | 4 | 3 | 4 | 5 | 5 | 4 | 5 | 4 | 5 | 71 |
| England | T14 | Round 2 | 4 | 4 | 3 | 3 | 4 | 4 | 4 | 3 | 4 | 4 | 4 | 5 | 3 | 4 | 3 | 4 | 4 | 4 | 68 |
| £196,000 | T6 | Round 3 | 4 | 4 | 3 | 4 | 4 | 4 | 4 | 3 | 3 | 3 | 3 | 4 | 5 | 4 | 4 | 4 | 4 | 3 | 68 |
| | T6 | Round 4 | 4 | 4 | 4 | 4 | 4 | 4 | 4 | 3 | 4 | 4 | 3 | 3 | 5 | 5 | 4 | 4 | 4 | 3 | 70-**277** |
| **Sergio Garcia** | T24 | Round 1 | 4 | 4 | 3 | 4 | 5 | 3 | 4 | 3 | 4 | 3 | 3 | 4 | 5 | 4 | 4 | 4 | 5 | 4 | 70 |
| Spain | T14 | Round 2 | 4 | 4 | 4 | 4 | 5 | 5 | 3 | 3 | 5 | 3 | 3 | 4 | 4 | 4 | 4 | 4 | 3 | 3 | 69 |
| £196,000 | T6 | Round 3 | 3 | 4 | 4 | 5 | 4 | 4 | 3 | 3 | 4 | 3 | 4 | 4 | 5 | 3 | 4 | 4 | 4 | 4 | 68 |
| | T6 | Round 4 | 3 | 4 | 3 | 4 | 4 | 4 | 3 | 3 | 4 | 3 | 3 | 5 | 5 | 5 | 4 | 4 | 5 | 4 | 70-**277** |

*Denotes amateur

| Player | Position | Round | 1 | 2 | 3 | 4 | 5 | 6 | 7 | 8 | 9 | 10 | 11 | 12 | 13 | 14 | 15 | 16 | 17 | 18 | TOTAL |
|---|---|---|---|---|---|---|---|---|---|---|---|---|---|---|---|---|---|---|---|---|---|
| **Jordan Niebrugge*** USA | T8 | Round 1 | 3 | 4 | 4 | 3 | 4 | 4 | 5 | 2 | 4 | 3 | 3 | 3 | 5 | 5 | 4 | 4 | 4 | 3 | 67 |
| | T21 | Round 2 | 4 | 5 | 3 | 6 | 4 | 4 | 4 | 3 | 4 | 5 | 3 | 4 | 4 | 4 | 4 | 4 | 4 | 4 | 73 |
| | T6 | Round 3 | 4 | 4 | 4 | 3 | 4 | 4 | 4 | 3 | 4 | 4 | 2 | 3 | 4 | 4 | 4 | 4 | 5 | 3 | 67 |
| | **T6** | Round 4 | 4 | 4 | 4 | 3 | 4 | 3 | 4 | 3 | 4 | 4 | 3 | 4 | 4 | 4 | 5 | 4 | 5 | 4 | 70-277 |
| **Brooks Koepka** USA £138,500 | T41 | Round 1 | 4 | 4 | 3 | 4 | 5 | 3 | 4 | 3 | 3 | 4 | 3 | 7 | 3 | 4 | 4 | 4 | 5 | 4 | 71 |
| | T25 | Round 2 | 4 | 4 | 4 | 5 | 4 | 4 | 3 | 3 | 4 | 3 | 4 | 4 | 4 | 4 | 3 | 4 | 5 | 4 | 70 |
| | T26 | Round 3 | 4 | 4 | 4 | 3 | 5 | 4 | 4 | 3 | 3 | 4 | 3 | 3 | 4 | 5 | 4 | 4 | 4 | 4 | 69 |
| | **T10** | Round 4 | 4 | 3 | 4 | 4 | 4 | 4 | 3 | 3 | 4 | 3 | 3 | 4 | 4 | 5 | 4 | 4 | 4 | 4 | 68-278 |
| **Adam Scott** Australia £138,500 | T24 | Round 1 | 4 | 4 | 3 | 5 | 4 | 4 | 4 | 3 | 4 | 3 | 3 | 5 | 4 | 5 | 5 | 3 | 4 | 3 | 70 |
| | T4 | Round 2 | 4 | 4 | 4 | 4 | 4 | 4 | 4 | 3 | 3 | 4 | 2 | 3 | 4 | 5 | 4 | 4 | 4 | 3 | 67 |
| | T6 | Round 3 | 4 | 4 | 4 | 4 | 4 | 4 | 4 | 3 | 4 | 4 | 2 | 4 | 3 | 5 | 4 | 4 | 5 | 4 | 70 |
| | **T10** | Round 4 | 3 | 4 | 4 | 4 | 4 | 3 | 3 | 3 | 3 | 3 | 3 | 4 | 4 | 6 | 5 | 4 | 5 | 6 | 71-278 |
| **Brendon Todd** USA £103,875 | T41 | Round 1 | 4 | 4 | 3 | 4 | 4 | 3 | 4 | 3 | 3 | 4 | 2 | 4 | 4 | 7 | 5 | 4 | 5 | 4 | 71 |
| | T61 | Round 2 | 3 | 5 | 4 | 4 | 4 | 4 | 4 | 2 | 4 | 4 | 4 | 4 | 4 | 5 | 4 | 5 | 5 | 4 | 73 |
| | T57 | Round 3 | 4 | 4 | 4 | 5 | 5 | 4 | 4 | 2 | 3 | 4 | 3 | 3 | 5 | 4 | 5 | 4 | 5 | 3 | 69 |
| | **T12** | Round 4 | 4 | 3 | 4 | 3 | 5 | 3 | 4 | 3 | 4 | 3 | 3 | 4 | 4 | 5 | 3 | 4 | 4 | 3 | 66-279 |
| **Oliver Schniederjans*** USA | T24 | Round 1 | 4 | 4 | 3 | 4 | 5 | 3 | 3 | 2 | 6 | 3 | 4 | 4 | 4 | 4 | 4 | 4 | 5 | 4 | 70 |
| | T39 | Round 2 | 4 | 5 | 5 | 5 | 4 | 4 | 4 | 3 | 4 | 3 | 3 | 3 | 4 | 5 | 4 | 4 | 5 | 3 | 72 |
| | T45 | Round 3 | 4 | 4 | 3 | 3 | 4 | 5 | 5 | 3 | 4 | 4 | 4 | 3 | 4 | 4 | 4 | 4 | 4 | 4 | 70 |
| | **T12** | Round 4 | 3 | 3 | 5 | 4 | 4 | 3 | 4 | 2 | 3 | 3 | 3 | 4 | 4 | 5 | 4 | 4 | 6 | 3 | 67-279 |
| **Luke Donald** England £103,875 | T13 | Round 1 | 4 | 4 | 3 | 4 | 4 | 3 | 4 | 2 | 4 | 4 | 3 | 4 | 4 | 5 | 4 | 4 | 4 | 4 | 68 |
| | T10 | Round 2 | 6 | 4 | 4 | 4 | 4 | 4 | 4 | 2 | 4 | 3 | 2 | 4 | 4 | 4 | 3 | 4 | 5 | 5 | 70 |
| | T33 | Round 3 | 4 | 5 | 4 | 4 | 5 | 4 | 4 | 3 | 3 | 4 | 3 | 4 | 4 | 5 | 5 | 4 | 4 | 4 | 73 |
| | **T12** | Round 4 | 3 | 4 | 4 | 3 | 5 | 4 | 4 | 3 | 4 | 3 | 2 | 3 | 4 | 5 | 4 | 4 | 5 | 4 | 68-279 |
| **Martin Kaymer** Germany £103,875 | T41 | Round 1 | 4 | 4 | 4 | 4 | 4 | 4 | 4 | 3 | 4 | 3 | 3 | 4 | 5 | 5 | 4 | 4 | 5 | 3 | 71 |
| | T25 | Round 2 | 4 | 3 | 5 | 4 | 4 | 4 | 4 | 3 | 4 | 3 | 4 | 4 | 5 | 4 | 4 | 4 | 4 | 3 | 70 |
| | T33 | Round 3 | 4 | 3 | 3 | 4 | 5 | 5 | 4 | 3 | 4 | 3 | 5 | 4 | 5 | 4 | 3 | 3 | 4 | 4 | 70 |
| | **T12** | Round 4 | 3 | 4 | 4 | 4 | 4 | 3 | 4 | 3 | 4 | 3 | 3 | 4 | 5 | 4 | 4 | 4 | 4 | 4 | 68-279 |
| **Ashley Chesters*** England | T41 | Round 1 | 4 | 4 | 3 | 4 | 4 | 3 | 4 | 3 | 4 | 2 | 3 | 4 | 4 | 5 | 4 | 5 | 5 | 6 | 71 |
| | T50 | Round 2 | 4 | 5 | 4 | 4 | 4 | 4 | 4 | 3 | 3 | 4 | 3 | 5 | 4 | 6 | 3 | 4 | 4 | 4 | 72 |
| | T26 | Round 3 | 4 | 3 | 3 | 4 | 3 | 4 | 4 | 2 | 4 | 4 | 3 | 4 | 4 | 5 | 4 | 4 | 5 | 3 | 67 |
| | **T12** | Round 4 | 4 | 3 | 3 | 4 | 5 | 3 | 4 | 3 | 3 | 3 | 3 | 4 | 4 | 5 | 6 | 4 | 4 | 4 | 69-279 |
| **Anthony Wall** England £103,875 | T24 | Round 1 | 4 | 4 | 4 | 4 | 4 | 4 | 3 | 3 | 4 | 3 | 4 | 4 | 5 | 5 | 4 | 4 | 4 | 4 | 70 |
| | T25 | Round 2 | 4 | 4 | 4 | 4 | 4 | 3 | 4 | 2 | 4 | 5 | 4 | 4 | 4 | 5 | 4 | 4 | 5 | 3 | 71 |
| | T18 | Round 3 | 3 | 4 | 4 | 4 | 4 | 4 | 4 | 3 | 4 | 2 | 4 | 5 | 5 | 3 | 4 | 4 | 4 | 4 | 68 |
| | **T12** | Round 4 | 3 | 4 | 3 | 4 | 4 | 4 | 3 | 3 | 4 | 2 | 4 | 5 | 6 | 4 | 5 | 4 | 4 | 4 | 70-279 |
| **Hideki Matsuyama** Japan £82,750 | T64 | Round 1 | 3 | 4 | 3 | 4 | 4 | 4 | 4 | 3 | 4 | 5 | 3 | 4 | 4 | 6 | 5 | 4 | 4 | 4 | 72 |
| | T10 | Round 2 | 3 | 3 | 3 | 3 | 5 | 4 | 3 | 3 | 3 | 3 | 4 | 5 | 4 | 4 | 4 | 4 | 4 | 4 | 66 |
| | T18 | Round 3 | 4 | 3 | 4 | 4 | 5 | 4 | 4 | 3 | 4 | 3 | 3 | 4 | 6 | 4 | 4 | 5 | 4 | | 71 |
| | **T18** | Round 4 | 3 | 4 | 4 | 4 | 4 | 3 | 3 | 4 | 3 | 4 | 3 | 3 | 5 | 4 | 5 | 5 | 5 | 4 | 71-280 |
| **Robert Streb** USA £82,750 | T2 | Round 1 | 3 | 4 | 3 | 4 | 4 | 3 | 4 | 3 | 5 | 3 | 5 | 3 | 4 | 5 | 3 | 4 | 4 | 4 | 66 |
| | T4 | Round 2 | 4 | 4 | 3 | 4 | 5 | 4 | 4 | 3 | 4 | 3 | 4 | 4 | 5 | 5 | 4 | 4 | 4 | 3 | 71 |
| | T6 | Round 3 | 4 | 3 | 4 | 4 | 4 | 5 | 4 | 3 | 4 | 3 | 3 | 5 | 4 | 4 | 4 | 4 | 4 | 4 | 70 |
| | **T18** | Round 4 | 4 | 4 | 4 | 4 | 5 | 3 | 4 | 3 | 4 | 3 | 4 | 4 | 4 | 6 | 4 | 4 | 5 | 4 | 73-280 |
| **Branden Grace** South Africa £61,475 | T18 | Round 1 | 4 | 4 | 4 | 4 | 3 | 4 | 2 | 4 | 3 | 3 | 4 | 4 | 5 | 4 | 4 | 5 | 4 | | 69 |
| | T25 | Round 2 | 4 | 4 | 3 | 4 | 5 | 4 | 4 | 3 | 3 | 4 | 3 | 4 | 5 | 5 | 4 | 5 | 4 | 4 | 72 |
| | T64 | Round 3 | 3 | 6 | 3 | 4 | 4 | 4 | 4 | 3 | 4 | 4 | 3 | 4 | 4 | 5 | 4 | 5 | 5 | 4 | 73 |
| | **T20** | Round 4 | 3 | 3 | 4 | 3 | 4 | 4 | 3 | 3 | 4 | 3 | 3 | 4 | 4 | 5 | 4 | 5 | 4 | 4 | 67-281 |

| HOLE | | | 1 | 2 | 3 | 4 | 5 | 6 | 7 | 8 | 9 | 10 | 11 | 12 | 13 | 14 | 15 | 16 | 17 | 18 | |
|---|---|---|---|---|---|---|---|---|---|---|---|---|---|---|---|---|---|---|---|---|---|
| **PAR** | **POSITION** | | 4 | 4 | 4 | 4 | 5 | 4 | 4 | 3 | 4 | 4 | 3 | 4 | 4 | 5 | 4 | 4 | 4 | 4 | **TOTAL** |
| **Russell Henley** | T109 | Round 1 | 4 | 6 | 4 | 4 | 5 | 4 | 4 | 3 | 4 | 3 | 3 | 4 | 4 | 6 | 5 | 3 | 4 | 4 | 74 |
| USA | T21 | Round 2 | 3 | 4 | 3 | 4 | 4 | 4 | 4 | 2 | 4 | 3 | 4 | 4 | 4 | 4 | 4 | 4 | 4 | 3 | 66 |
| £61,475 | T45 | Round 3 | 3 | 4 | 4 | 5 | 4 | 4 | 4 | 3 | 4 | 4 | 2 | 6 | 3 | 4 | 5 | 4 | 5 | 4 | 72 |
| | **T20** | Round 4 | 4 | 3 | 4 | 4 | 5 | 4 | 3 | 3 | 4 | 3 | 3 | 4 | 4 | 5 | 4 | 4 | 4 | 4 | 69 -**281** |
| **Greg Owen** | T13 | Round 1 | 3 | 4 | 4 | 4 | 5 | 3 | 4 | 3 | 3 | 4 | 3 | 4 | 5 | 4 | 4 | 4 | 4 | 3 | 68 |
| England | T25 | Round 2 | 6 | 4 | 4 | 5 | 3 | 4 | 4 | 3 | 4 | 4 | 3 | 4 | 4 | 5 | 4 | 4 | 5 | 3 | 73 |
| £61,475 | T45 | Round 3 | 4 | 4 | 4 | 4 | 5 | 4 | 3 | 4 | 4 | 5 | 2 | 4 | 4 | 5 | 4 | 4 | 4 | 3 | 71 |
| | **T20** | Round 4 | 5 | 3 | 4 | 4 | 5 | 3 | 4 | 3 | 4 | 3 | 3 | 4 | 4 | 5 | 4 | 4 | 4 | 3 | 69 -**281** |
| **Phil Mickelson** | T24 | Round 1 | 4 | 3 | 4 | 3 | 4 | 5 | 4 | 4 | 4 | 3 | 3 | 4 | 4 | 5 | 4 | 4 | 5 | 3 | 70 |
| USA | T39 | Round 2 | 4 | 4 | 3 | 4 | 4 | 4 | 4 | 3 | 4 | 3 | 5 | 4 | 3 | 5 | 5 | 4 | 4 | 5 | 72 |
| £61,475 | T45 | Round 3 | 5 | 4 | 3 | 4 | 4 | 4 | 4 | 3 | 3 | 4 | 3 | 4 | 4 | 5 | 4 | 4 | 5 | 3 | 70 |
| | **T20** | Round 4 | 3 | 4 | 4 | 4 | 5 | 3 | 3 | 3 | 4 | 3 | 3 | 4 | 4 | 4 | 3 | 4 | 7 | 4 | 69 -**281** |
| **James Morrison** | T41 | Round 1 | 5 | 4 | 4 | 4 | 4 | 4 | 3 | 2 | 4 | 3 | 3 | 4 | 4 | 5 | 4 | 5 | 5 | 4 | 71 |
| England | T39 | Round 2 | 4 | 4 | 4 | 4 | 4 | 4 | 3 | 3 | 3 | 4 | 3 | 4 | 5 | 5 | 4 | 5 | 5 | 3 | 71 |
| £61,475 | T45 | Round 3 | 4 | 4 | 4 | 4 | 4 | 5 | 4 | 3 | 3 | 3 | 3 | 4 | 3 | 6 | 4 | 4 | 4 | 4 | 70 |
| | **T20** | Round 4 | 4 | 4 | 4 | 4 | 4 | 3 | 4 | 3 | 4 | 3 | 3 | 4 | 5 | 4 | 4 | 4 | 4 | 4 | 69 -**281** |
| **Marcus Fraser** | T109 | Round 1 | 5 | 4 | 4 | 5 | 4 | 3 | 3 | 4 | 4 | 4 | 4 | 4 | 4 | 5 | 4 | 4 | 4 | 5 | 74 |
| Australia | T50 | Round 2 | 4 | 4 | 3 | 5 | 4 | 5 | 3 | 3 | 4 | 4 | 3 | 3 | 4 | 5 | 4 | 4 | 4 | 3 | 69 |
| £61,475 | T33 | Round 3 | 4 | 4 | 4 | 4 | 4 | 4 | 4 | 4 | 3 | 3 | 2 | 4 | 4 | 4 | 4 | 4 | 4 | 4 | 68 |
| | **T20** | Round 4 | 3 | 4 | 4 | 4 | 4 | 3 | 4 | 3 | 3 | 4 | 2 | 4 | 5 | 6 | 4 | 4 | 5 | 4 | 70 -**281** |
| **Stewart Cink** | T24 | Round 1 | 4 | 4 | 3 | 4 | 5 | 3 | 4 | 3 | 4 | 4 | 3 | 3 | 5 | 4 | 4 | 4 | 5 | 4 | 70 |
| USA | T25 | Round 2 | 4 | 4 | 4 | 4 | 5 | 4 | 3 | 3 | 4 | 4 | 4 | 4 | 4 | 4 | 4 | 4 | 5 | 3 | 71 |
| £61,475 | T18 | Round 3 | 3 | 4 | 4 | 5 | 5 | 4 | 3 | 3 | 4 | 2 | 4 | 4 | 4 | 4 | 4 | 4 | 4 | 3 | 68 |
| | **T20** | Round 4 | 4 | 3 | 4 | 4 | 4 | 4 | 4 | 3 | 3 | 3 | 4 | 4 | 5 | 6 | 4 | 5 | 4 | 4 | 72 -**281** |
| **Patrick Reed** | T64 | Round 1 | 5 | 4 | 4 | 4 | 4 | 5 | 3 | 4 | 4 | 4 | 4 | 4 | 4 | 4 | 4 | 3 | 4 | 4 | 72 |
| USA | T39 | Round 2 | 3 | 3 | 4 | 4 | 4 | 4 | 3 | 3 | 4 | 4 | 3 | 3 | 4 | 6 | 4 | 4 | 5 | 4 | 70 |
| £61,475 | T18 | Round 3 | 4 | 5 | 4 | 4 | 5 | 3 | 3 | 3 | 4 | 2 | 3 | 3 | 5 | 4 | 4 | 4 | 4 | 3 | 67 |
| | **T20** | Round 4 | 4 | 4 | 4 | 4 | 5 | 4 | 3 | 3 | 4 | 3 | 3 | 5 | 4 | 6 | 4 | 4 | 4 | 4 | 72 -**281** |
| **Retief Goosen** | T2 | Round 1 | 3 | 3 | 5 | 4 | 4 | 4 | 4 | 2 | 4 | 3 | 4 | 3 | 3 | 4 | 5 | 4 | 4 | 3 | 66 |
| South Africa | T10 | Round 2 | 4 | 5 | 4 | 4 | 5 | 4 | 4 | 3 | 3 | 4 | 4 | 3 | 3 | 5 | 4 | 5 | 4 | 4 | 72 |
| £61,475 | T6 | Round 3 | 4 | 4 | 4 | 4 | 3 | 3 | 4 | 3 | 4 | 4 | 3 | 4 | 3 | 5 | 4 | 4 | 5 | 4 | 69 |
| | **T20** | Round 4 | 4 | 4 | 4 | 5 | 4 | 5 | 4 | 3 | 4 | 4 | 3 | 4 | 4 | 5 | 4 | 4 | 5 | 4 | 74 -**281** |
| **Padraig Harrington** | T64 | Round 1 | 4 | 4 | 5 | 4 | 4 | 3 | 4 | 3 | 4 | 4 | 4 | 3 | 4 | 5 | 4 | 4 | 5 | 4 | 72 |
| Republic of Ireland | T25 | Round 2 | 4 | 5 | 4 | 4 | 5 | 4 | 3 | 3 | 4 | 4 | 3 | 4 | 3 | 4 | 4 | 4 | 4 | 3 | 69 |
| £61,475 | 5 | Round 3 | 3 | 4 | 3 | 4 | 4 | 4 | 3 | 3 | 3 | 3 | 3 | 4 | 4 | 5 | 4 | 3 | 4 | 4 | 65 |
| | **T20** | Round 4 | 3 | 3 | 4 | 4 | 4 | 6 | 4 | 4 | 4 | 4 | 2 | 4 | 4 | 6 | 5 | 3 | 6 | 5 | 75 -**281** |
| **Billy Horschel** | T87 | Round 1 | 4 | 4 | 4 | 4 | 5 | 4 | 3 | 3 | 4 | 2 | 4 | 4 | 6 | 4 | 5 | 4 | 5 | 4 | 73 |
| USA | T61 | Round 2 | 4 | 3 | 4 | 4 | 4 | 5 | 4 | 3 | 5 | 3 | 3 | 4 | 5 | 5 | 4 | 5 | 3 | 3 | 71 |
| £40,417 | T70 | Round 3 | 4 | 4 | 4 | 5 | 4 | 4 | 3 | 3 | 4 | 4 | 3 | 3 | 3 | 5 | 5 | 5 | 4 | 4 | 71 |
| | **T30** | Round 4 | 4 | 4 | 4 | 4 | 4 | 3 | 4 | 4 | 3 | 4 | 2 | 3 | 5 | 4 | 4 | 4 | 3 | 4 | 67 -**282** |
| **Jimmy Walker** | T64 | Round 1 | 3 | 4 | 4 | 5 | 4 | 3 | 3 | 3 | 4 | 4 | 3 | 5 | 4 | 5 | 4 | 5 | 5 | 4 | 72 |
| USA | T21 | Round 2 | 4 | 4 | 4 | 3 | 4 | 4 | 4 | 3 | 3 | 4 | 3 | 3 | 4 | 5 | 5 | 4 | 4 | 3 | 68 |
| £40,417 | T33 | Round 3 | 4 | 3 | 4 | 5 | 5 | 3 | 4 | 3 | 4 | 4 | 3 | 4 | 4 | 4 | 4 | 4 | 5 | 4 | 71 |
| | **T30** | Round 4 | 4 | 4 | 4 | 5 | 3 | 4 | 5 | 3 | 4 | 3 | 3 | 3 | 4 | 6 | 4 | 4 | 5 | 4 | 71 -**282** |
| **Andy Sullivan** | T64 | Round 1 | 4 | 3 | 4 | 5 | 4 | 4 | 3 | 3 | 4 | 3 | 3 | 4 | 5 | 6 | 4 | 4 | 4 | 5 | 72 |
| England | T50 | Round 2 | 3 | 4 | 4 | 4 | 4 | 4 | 3 | 3 | 5 | 4 | 4 | 4 | 5 | 4 | 4 | 4 | 5 | 3 | 71 |
| £40,417 | T33 | Round 3 | 4 | 6 | 4 | 4 | 4 | 3 | 4 | 3 | 3 | 4 | 3 | 3 | 4 | 3 | 4 | 4 | 3 | 5 | 68 |
| | **T30** | Round 4 | 3 | 3 | 3 | 3 | 7 | 4 | 3 | 3 | 4 | 3 | 3 | 4 | 4 | 7 | 5 | 4 | 4 | 4 | 71 -**282** |

| HOLE | | | 1 | 2 | 3 | 4 | 5 | 6 | 7 | 8 | 9 | 10 | 11 | 12 | 13 | 14 | 15 | 16 | 17 | 18 | |
|---|---|---|---|---|---|---|---|---|---|---|---|---|---|---|---|---|---|---|---|---|---|
| PAR | POSITION | | 4 | 4 | 4 | 4 | 5 | 4 | 4 | 3 | 4 | 4 | 3 | 4 | 4 | 5 | 4 | 4 | 4 | 4 | TOTAL |
| **Anirban Lahiri** | T18 | Round 1 | 3 | 3 | 4 | 4 | 5 | 4 | 3 | 3 | 4 | 4 | 3 | 4 | 5 | 4 | 3 | 4 | 5 | 4 | 69 |
| India | T14 | Round 2 | 3 | 4 | 4 | 4 | 5 | 4 | 4 | 3 | 4 | 4 | 3 | 4 | 4 | 4 | 4 | 4 | 4 | 4 | 70 |
| £40,417 | T26 | Round 3 | 3 | 4 | 4 | 3 | 5 | 4 | 4 | 3 | 3 | 4 | 2 | 4 | 5 | 6 | 4 | 4 | 5 | 4 | 71 |
| | **T30** | Round 4 | 5 | 4 | 4 | 3 | 4 | 4 | 3 | 3 | 3 | 4 | 3 | 4 | 5 | 5 | 5 | 5 | 5 | 3 | 72 -**282** |
| **Matt Jones** | T13 | Round 1 | 4 | 3 | 4 | 4 | 4 | 4 | 5 | 3 | 4 | 4 | 2 | 4 | 4 | 5 | 3 | 4 | 4 | 3 | 68 |
| Australia | T25 | Round 2 | 4 | 5 | 4 | 3 | 6 | 4 | 4 | 4 | 4 | 4 | 3 | 4 | 4 | 4 | 4 | 4 | 4 | 4 | 73 |
| £40,417 | T26 | Round 3 | 3 | 4 | 4 | 3 | 4 | 4 | 4 | 3 | 4 | 4 | 3 | 4 | 4 | 5 | 4 | 4 | 5 | 3 | 69 |
| | **T30** | Round 4 | 3 | 6 | 5 | 4 | 4 | 3 | 4 | 3 | 4 | 4 | 2 | 5 | 4 | 6 | 4 | 4 | 5 | 2 | 72 -**282** |
| **Jim Furyk** | T87 | Round 1 | 4 | 3 | 4 | 4 | 5 | 4 | 4 | 3 | 4 | 4 | 2 | 4 | 5 | 7 | 5 | 3 | 5 | 3 | 73 |
| USA | T61 | Round 2 | 3 | 4 | 3 | 4 | 4 | 4 | 4 | 3 | 4 | 4 | 3 | 5 | 4 | 5 | 5 | 4 | 5 | 3 | 71 |
| £40,417 | T26 | Round 3 | 4 | 4 | 4 | 4 | 4 | 3 | 4 | 2 | 3 | 4 | 3 | 3 | 4 | 5 | 3 | 4 | 4 | 4 | 66 |
| | **T30** | Round 4 | 4 | 4 | 4 | 3 | 4 | 4 | 5 | 3 | 4 | 4 | 3 | 4 | 4 | 4 | 5 | 4 | 5 | 4 | 72 -**282** |
| **Ryan Palmer** | T41 | Round 1 | 4 | 4 | 4 | 4 | 4 | 4 | 4 | 3 | 4 | 4 | 4 | 3 | 3 | 5 | 4 | 4 | 5 | 4 | 71 |
| USA | T39 | Round 2 | 4 | 4 | 4 | 6 | 5 | 4 | 4 | 3 | 4 | 4 | 4 | 3 | 4 | 4 | 4 | 3 | 4 | 3 | 71 |
| £40,417 | T18 | Round 3 | 4 | 4 | 3 | 4 | 5 | 5 | 4 | 3 | 3 | 3 | 3 | 3 | 4 | 4 | 4 | 4 | 4 | 3 | 67 |
| | **T30** | Round 4 | 4 | 4 | 4 | 4 | 4 | 4 | 4 | 3 | 4 | 3 | 3 | 4 | 5 | 5 | 5 | 4 | 5 | 4 | 73 -**282** |
| **Rickie Fowler** | T64 | Round 1 | 4 | 4 | 4 | 4 | 5 | 4 | 4 | 4 | 4 | 4 | 2 | 3 | 4 | 5 | 5 | 4 | 4 | 4 | 72 |
| USA | T50 | Round 2 | 4 | 4 | 4 | 4 | 4 | 4 | 4 | 3 | 4 | 4 | 3 | 4 | 4 | 5 | 4 | 4 | 5 | 3 | 71 |
| £40,417 | T18 | Round 3 | 4 | 4 | 4 | 3 | 4 | 4 | 3 | 3 | 4 | 4 | 2 | 4 | 3 | 5 | 3 | 4 | 5 | 3 | 66 |
| | **T30** | Round 4 | 3 | 5 | 5 | 4 | 4 | 4 | 4 | 3 | 4 | 4 | 3 | 4 | 5 | 5 | 4 | 4 | 5 | 3 | 73 -**282** |
| **Steven Bowditch** | T24 | Round 1 | 4 | 3 | 3 | 4 | 4 | 4 | 4 | 2 | 5 | 3 | 4 | 3 | 4 | 5 | 4 | 4 | 5 | 5 | 70 |
| Australia | T14 | Round 2 | 4 | 4 | 4 | 4 | 4 | 4 | 4 | 3 | 5 | 3 | 3 | 3 | 3 | 5 | 4 | 4 | 5 | 3 | 69 |
| £40,417 | T15 | Round 3 | 3 | 4 | 3 | 4 | 4 | 4 | 3 | 3 | 4 | 3 | 3 | 5 | 6 | 4 | 4 | 4 | 4 | 4 | 69 |
| | **T30** | Round 4 | 5 | 4 | 4 | 4 | 4 | 4 | 4 | 3 | 4 | 3 | 4 | 4 | 5 | 5 | 4 | 5 | 4 | 4 | 74 -**282** |
| **Paul Dunne*** | T18 | Round 1 | 3 | 3 | 4 | 4 | 4 | 4 | 4 | 3 | 4 | 4 | 4 | 4 | 5 | 4 | 4 | 4 | 4 | 4 | 69 |
| Republic of Ireland | T10 | Round 2 | 4 | 4 | 4 | 4 | 5 | 4 | 3 | 3 | 3 | 4 | 3 | 4 | 4 | 4 | 3 | 5 | 4 | 3 | 69 |
| | T1 | Round 3 | 3 | 4 | 4 | 3 | 5 | 4 | 3 | 3 | 3 | 3 | 3 | 4 | 5 | 3 | 4 | 4 | 4 | 4 | 66 |
| | **T30** | Round 4 | 5 | 5 | 3 | 4 | 4 | 4 | 3 | 3 | 4 | 5 | 3 | 5 | 6 | 5 | 4 | 4 | 5 | 5 | 78 -**282** |
| **Scott Arnold** | T41 | Round 1 | 4 | 4 | 4 | 4 | 4 | 3 | 3 | 4 | 3 | 3 | 4 | 7 | 4 | 4 | 4 | 4 | 71 |
| Australia | T61 | Round 2 | 4 | 5 | 4 | 5 | 6 | 4 | 4 | 3 | 5 | 4 | 3 | 3 | 3 | 4 | 3 | 4 | 5 | 4 | 73 |
| £27,861 | T78 | Round 3 | 4 | 4 | 4 | 5 | 5 | 4 | 4 | 3 | 4 | 3 | 3 | 4 | 4 | 5 | 4 | 4 | 5 | 4 | 73 |
| | **T40** | Round 4 | 3 | 4 | 4 | 3 | 5 | 3 | 4 | 3 | 3 | 4 | 2 | 4 | 3 | 5 | 4 | 4 | 4 | 4 | 66 -**283** |
| **Francesco Molinari** | T64 | Round 1 | 4 | 5 | 4 | 4 | 4 | 3 | 4 | 3 | 4 | 3 | 5 | 4 | 5 | 4 | 4 | 5 | 3 | 72 |
| Italy | T50 | Round 2 | 4 | 4 | 3 | 5 | 4 | 4 | 4 | 3 | 4 | 3 | 3 | 5 | 4 | 5 | 4 | 4 | 5 | 3 | 71 |
| £27,861 | T74 | Round 3 | 4 | 4 | 5 | 5 | 5 | 4 | 4 | 3 | 4 | 3 | 4 | 5 | 5 | 4 | 4 | 5 | 3 | 73 |
| | **T40** | Round 4 | 3 | 4 | 4 | 4 | 3 | 3 | 4 | 3 | 3 | 3 | 3 | 4 | 4 | 5 | 4 | 4 | 5 | 4 | 67 -**283** |
| **Henrik Stenson** | T87 | Round 1 | 4 | 4 | 4 | 4 | 4 | 3 | 4 | 4 | 4 | 3 | 4 | 4 | 5 | 5 | 4 | 4 | 5 | 4 | 73 |
| Sweden | T50 | Round 2 | 3 | 3 | 3 | 4 | 4 | 4 | 4 | 3 | 4 | 5 | 3 | 5 | 4 | 5 | 4 | 4 | 4 | 4 | 70 |
| £27,861 | T64 | Round 3 | 3 | 4 | 4 | 5 | 4 | 4 | 4 | 3 | 4 | 4 | 2 | 4 | 4 | 5 | 4 | 4 | 5 | 4 | 71 |
| | **T40** | Round 4 | 4 | 5 | 4 | 3 | 4 | 4 | 3 | 3 | 4 | 3 | 3 | 4 | 4 | 5 | 4 | 4 | 5 | 3 | 69 -**283** |
| **Rafa Cabrera-Bello** | T41 | Round 1 | 4 | 3 | 3 | 4 | 4 | 3 | 3 | 3 | 4 | 4 | 3 | 4 | 5 | 6 | 5 | 4 | 5 | 4 | 71 |
| Spain | T61 | Round 2 | 3 | 5 | 3 | 4 | 5 | 4 | 4 | 3 | 4 | 4 | 4 | 4 | 4 | 5 | 4 | 4 | 5 | 4 | 73 |
| £27,861 | T45 | Round 3 | 3 | 4 | 3 | 5 | 4 | 5 | 4 | 3 | 4 | 4 | 2 | 3 | 4 | 4 | 4 | 5 | 4 | 68 |
| | **T40** | Round 4 | 5 | 5 | 3 | 4 | 4 | 3 | 4 | 4 | 3 | 4 | 4 | 3 | 3 | 5 | 4 | 5 | 5 | 4 | 71 -**283** |
| **John Senden** | T64 | Round 1 | 4 | 4 | 4 | 4 | 4 | 4 | 3 | 4 | 5 | 2 | 4 | 4 | 5 | 5 | 4 | 4 | 4 | 72 |
| Australia | T61 | Round 2 | 4 | 4 | 4 | 5 | 6 | 4 | 3 | 3 | 4 | 4 | 3 | 3 | 5 | 4 | 4 | 4 | 4 | 4 | 72 |
| £27,861 | T45 | Round 3 | 3 | 5 | 4 | 5 | 4 | 4 | 3 | 2 | 4 | 4 | 3 | 4 | 3 | 4 | 4 | 4 | 5 | 3 | 68 |
| | **T40** | Round 4 | 3 | 5 | 5 | 4 | 4 | 3 | 3 | 3 | 4 | 4 | 3 | 5 | 4 | 5 | 4 | 4 | 4 | 4 | 71 -**283** |

| HOLE | | | 1 | 2 | 3 | 4 | 5 | 6 | 7 | 8 | 9 | 10 | 11 | 12 | 13 | 14 | 15 | 16 | 17 | 18 | |
|---|---|---|---|---|---|---|---|---|---|---|---|---|---|---|---|---|---|---|---|---|---|
| PAR | POSITION | | 4 | 4 | 4 | 4 | 5 | 4 | 4 | 3 | 4 | 4 | 3 | 4 | 4 | 5 | 4 | 4 | 4 | 4 | TOTAL |
| **Geoff Ogilvy** | T41 | Round 1 | 3 | 3 | 4 | 4 | 4 | 3 | 4 | 3 | 4 | 3 | 3 | 3 | 5 | 7 | 5 | 5 | 4 | 4 | 71 |
| Australia | T14 | Round 2 | 4 | 4 | 4 | 5 | 5 | 3 | 3 | 3 | 4 | 4 | 3 | 4 | 4 | 5 | 3 | 4 | 3 | 3 | 68 |
| £27,861 | T33 | Round 3 | 3 | 4 | 5 | 4 | 5 | 3 | 5 | 3 | 4 | 3 | 2 | 4 | 4 | 5 | 4 | 5 | 5 | 4 | 72 |
| | **T40** | Round 4 | 4 | 3 | 3 | 4 | 4 | 4 | 4 | 3 | 4 | 4 | 3 | 4 | 5 | 6 | 4 | 5 | 5 | 3 | 72-**283** |
| **Webb Simpson** | T24 | Round 1 | 4 | 4 | 4 | 4 | 4 | 4 | 3 | 3 | 3 | 4 | 4 | 4 | 4 | 4 | 4 | 4 | 5 | 4 | 70 |
| USA | T21 | Round 2 | 4 | 4 | 4 | 3 | 5 | 3 | 3 | 4 | 5 | 3 | 3 | 3 | 5 | 5 | 4 | 5 | 4 | 3 | 70 |
| £27,861 | T33 | Round 3 | 3 | 5 | 4 | 5 | 4 | 5 | 4 | 3 | 3 | 4 | 2 | 4 | 4 | 5 | 4 | 5 | 4 | 3 | 71 |
| | **T40** | Round 4 | 4 | 4 | 4 | 5 | 4 | 4 | 4 | 3 | 4 | 3 | 3 | 4 | 5 | 5 | 4 | 4 | 5 | 3 | 72-**283** |
| **Paul Lawrie** | T2 | Round 1 | 4 | 3 | 4 | 4 | 4 | 3 | 3 | 3 | 3 | 4 | 3 | 3 | 3 | 5 | 4 | 4 | 5 | 4 | 66 |
| Scotland | 3 | Round 2 | 4 | 4 | 3 | 5 | 5 | 4 | 3 | 3 | 4 | 3 | 3 | 4 | 4 | 5 | 4 | 4 | 4 | 4 | 70 |
| £27,861 | T26 | Round 3 | 4 | 4 | 3 | 4 | 5 | 5 | 4 | 3 | 4 | 4 | 2 | 4 | 5 | 5 | 4 | 4 | 6 | 4 | 74 |
| | **T40** | Round 4 | 5 | 3 | 4 | 4 | 4 | 4 | 4 | 3 | 4 | 4 | 3 | 4 | 5 | 5 | 4 | 4 | 5 | 4 | 73-**283** |
| **Marc Warren** | T13 | Round 1 | 4 | 4 | 3 | 4 | 4 | 4 | 3 | 2 | 4 | 4 | 4 | 4 | 3 | 4 | 4 | 5 | 4 | 4 | 68 |
| Scotland | T4 | Round 2 | 4 | 4 | 4 | 3 | 4 | 4 | 3 | 4 | 4 | 3 | 4 | 4 | 4 | 5 | 4 | 4 | 4 | 3 | 69 |
| £27,861 | T18 | Round 3 | 4 | 3 | 4 | 4 | 5 | 4 | 4 | 3 | 4 | 2 | 4 | 5 | 4 | 5 | 5 | 4 | 4 | 4 | 72 |
| | **T40** | Round 4 | 4 | 4 | 5 | 5 | 5 | 4 | 3 | 3 | 4 | 3 | 4 | 5 | 4 | 5 | 4 | 4 | 4 | 4 | 74-**283** |
| **Ryan Fox** | T64 | Round 1 | 3 | 4 | 5 | 5 | 4 | 4 | 4 | 2 | 4 | 3 | 3 | 3 | 4 | 6 | 5 | 4 | 5 | 4 | 72 |
| New Zealand | T25 | Round 2 | 4 | 4 | 4 | 4 | 5 | 4 | 4 | 4 | 4 | 3 | 4 | 4 | 4 | 3 | 4 | 3 | 4 | 3 | 69 |
| £18,728 | T78 | Round 3 | 4 | 6 | 4 | 5 | 5 | 5 | 4 | 3 | 4 | 3 | 3 | 4 | 4 | 5 | 4 | 5 | 5 | 3 | 76 |
| | **T49** | Round 4 | 3 | 3 | 4 | 4 | 5 | 4 | 4 | 3 | 3 | 3 | 3 | 4 | 3 | 5 | 4 | 5 | 4 | 3 | 67-**284** |
| **David Howell** | T13 | Round 1 | 3 | 4 | 4 | 4 | 5 | 3 | 3 | 2 | 4 | 4 | 3 | 3 | 4 | 5 | 4 | 4 | 5 | 4 | 68 |
| England | T25 | Round 2 | 4 | 4 | 4 | 4 | 5 | 4 | 5 | 4 | 3 | 4 | 3 | 4 | 4 | 5 | 4 | 4 | 4 | 4 | 73 |
| £18,728 | T64 | Round 3 | 4 | 5 | 4 | 4 | 5 | 5 | 4 | 3 | 4 | 3 | 2 | 5 | 4 | 5 | 4 | 4 | 4 | 4 | 73 |
| | **T49** | Round 4 | 4 | 3 | 4 | 4 | 5 | 3 | 3 | 3 | 4 | 3 | 3 | 4 | 4 | 6 | 4 | 4 | 6 | 3 | 70-**284** |
| **Jamie Donaldson** | T64 | Round 1 | 4 | 4 | 4 | 4 | 4 | 4 | 5 | 3 | 3 | 3 | 3 | 4 | 5 | 4 | 4 | 4 | 6 | 4 | 72 |
| Wales | T50 | Round 2 | 4 | 4 | 4 | 4 | 4 | 4 | 4 | 3 | 3 | 4 | 4 | 4 | 4 | 5 | 4 | 4 | 4 | 4 | 71 |
| £18,728 | T64 | Round 3 | 4 | 5 | 3 | 4 | 4 | 4 | 3 | 3 | 4 | 4 | 3 | 5 | 4 | 5 | 4 | 4 | 4 | 4 | 71 |
| | **T49** | Round 4 | 4 | 4 | 3 | 4 | 4 | 3 | 3 | 3 | 3 | 3 | 3 | 5 | 4 | 5 | 4 | 5 | 7 | 3 | 70-**284** |
| **Graeme McDowell** | T64 | Round 1 | 4 | 4 | 4 | 4 | 5 | 4 | 4 | 3 | 4 | 3 | 2 | 5 | 4 | 5 | 4 | 5 | 4 | 4 | 72 |
| Northern Ireland | T61 | Round 2 | 4 | 4 | 4 | 5 | 5 | 4 | 3 | 3 | 4 | 4 | 3 | 4 | 3 | 4 | 4 | 4 | 6 | 4 | 72 |
| £18,728 | T64 | Round 3 | 3 | 4 | 3 | 3 | 4 | 6 | 3 | 3 | 3 | 5 | 2 | 4 | 3 | 7 | 5 | 4 | 4 | 4 | 70 |
| | **T49** | Round 4 | 3 | 4 | 4 | 4 | 4 | 4 | 3 | 3 | 3 | 4 | 3 | 3 | 5 | 5 | 3 | 4 | 5 | 5 | 70-**284** |
| **Lee Westwood** | T41 | Round 1 | 3 | 4 | 5 | 4 | 4 | 3 | 3 | 3 | 4 | 4 | 4 | 3 | 4 | 4 | 4 | 5 | 5 | 5 | 71 |
| England | T61 | Round 2 | 4 | 5 | 4 | 4 | 4 | 4 | 3 | 4 | 4 | 3 | 3 | 5 | 3 | 4 | 4 | 6 | 5 | 4 | 73 |
| £18,728 | T57 | Round 3 | 4 | 4 | 4 | 4 | 5 | 4 | 3 | 3 | 3 | 4 | 3 | 4 | 4 | 4 | 4 | 4 | 5 | 3 | 69 |
| | **T49** | Round 4 | 4 | 5 | 4 | 4 | 4 | 4 | 3 | 3 | 3 | 3 | 3 | 4 | 5 | 5 | 4 | 4 | 4 | 4 | 71-**284** |
| **Hunter Mahan** | T64 | Round 1 | 3 | 4 | 3 | 4 | 4 | 3 | 4 | 3 | 4 | 4 | 3 | 4 | 5 | 5 | 5 | 5 | 5 | 4 | 72 |
| USA | T61 | Round 2 | 3 | 4 | 4 | 4 | 5 | 4 | 4 | 3 | 4 | 5 | 3 | 3 | 4 | 4 | 5 | 4 | 6 | 3 | 72 |
| £18,728 | T33 | Round 3 | 4 | 3 | 4 | 4 | 4 | 5 | 3 | 3 | 3 | 4 | 2 | 4 | 4 | 5 | 4 | 4 | 4 | 3 | 67 |
| | **T49** | Round 4 | 4 | 4 | 4 | 5 | 4 | 4 | 4 | 3 | 4 | 3 | 2 | 4 | 4 | 6 | 4 | 5 | 5 | 4 | 73-**284** |
| **David Duval** | T64 | Round 1 | 3 | 4 | 3 | 5 | 4 | 4 | 4 | 3 | 4 | 4 | 5 | 4 | 3 | 4 | 4 | 4 | 6 | 4 | 72 |
| USA | T61 | Round 2 | 4 | 5 | 3 | 4 | 5 | 4 | 4 | 3 | 4 | 4 | 4 | 3 | 4 | 5 | 4 | 4 | 5 | 3 | 72 |
| £18,728 | T33 | Round 3 | 4 | 3 | 4 | 4 | 4 | 4 | 3 | 3 | 3 | 5 | 2 | 4 | 3 | 4 | 4 | 5 | 4 | 4 | 67 |
| | **T49** | Round 4 | 4 | 5 | 3 | 5 | 4 | 4 | 3 | 3 | 4 | 3 | 3 | 3 | 5 | 6 | 4 | 4 | 6 | 4 | 73-**284** |
| **Dustin Johnson** | 1 | Round 1 | 4 | 3 | 3 | 4 | 3 | 4 | 3 | 3 | 3 | 3 | 3 | 4 | 4 | 4 | 4 | 4 | 4 | 4 | 65 |
| USA | 1 | Round 2 | 4 | 4 | 4 | 3 | 4 | 4 | 3 | 3 | 4 | 3 | 4 | 4 | 4 | 6 | 4 | 4 | 4 | 3 | 69 |
| £18,728 | T18 | Round 3 | 4 | 4 | 4 | 4 | 5 | 4 | 5 | 3 | 4 | 4 | 3 | 4 | 4 | 5 | 3 | 5 | 5 | 5 | 75 |
| | **T49** | Round 4 | 3 | 5 | 5 | 5 | 4 | 5 | 4 | 4 | 4 | 3 | 3 | 4 | 4 | 5 | 4 | 4 | 6 | 3 | 75-**284** |

| HOLE | | | 1 | 2 | 3 | 4 | 5 | 6 | 7 | 8 | 9 | 10 | 11 | 12 | 13 | 14 | 15 | 16 | 17 | 18 | |
|---|---|---|---|---|---|---|---|---|---|---|---|---|---|---|---|---|---|---|---|---|---|
| PAR | POSITION | | 4 | 4 | 4 | 4 | 5 | 4 | 4 | 3 | 4 | 4 | 3 | 4 | 4 | 5 | 4 | 4 | 4 | 4 | TOTAL |
| **Eddie Pepperell** | T64 | Round 1 | 3 | 4 | 4 | 4 | 6 | 3 | 4 | 3 | 4 | 4 | 4 | 3 | 4 | 5 | 4 | 4 | 5 | 4 | 72 |
| England | T39 | Round 2 | 4 | 4 | 4 | 3 | 5 | 4 | 4 | 3 | 4 | 3 | 3 | 4 | 3 | 6 | 4 | 4 | 4 | 4 | 70 |
| £18,728 | T15 | Round 3 | 3 | 3 | 4 | 3 | 4 | 3 | 4 | 3 | 4 | 3 | 3 | 4 | 4 | 5 | 3 | 3 | 6 | 4 | 66 |
| | **T49** | Round 4 | 4 | 3 | 4 | 5 | 5 | 4 | 4 | 3 | 4 | 3 | 3 | 4 | 5 | 6 | 5 | 4 | 6 | 4 | 76-**284** |
| **Cameron Tringale** | T41 | Round 1 | 3 | 3 | 3 | 4 | 4 | 4 | 3 | 3 | 4 | 4 | 3 | 4 | 4 | 5 | 4 | 7 | 5 | 4 | 71 |
| USA | T39 | Round 2 | 4 | 4 | 4 | 4 | 4 | 4 | 4 | 3 | 4 | 3 | 3 | 5 | 4 | 5 | 4 | 4 | 5 | 3 | 71 |
| £15,907 | T70 | Round 3 | 3 | 4 | 4 | 4 | 4 | 4 | 4 | 3 | 4 | 4 | 3 | 4 | 3 | 5 | 4 | 5 | 7 | 4 | 73 |
| | **T58** | Round 4 | 4 | 4 | 4 | 4 | 5 | 4 | 4 | 2 | 3 | 3 | 3 | 4 | 4 | 5 | 4 | 5 | 4 | 4 | 70-**285** |
| **Matt Kuchar** | T41 | Round 1 | 4 | 4 | 4 | 5 | 4 | 3 | 3 | 4 | 4 | 3 | 3 | 4 | 4 | 5 | 4 | 4 | 5 | 4 | 71 |
| USA | T61 | Round 2 | 4 | 5 | 4 | 4 | 4 | 3 | 4 | 4 | 3 | 3 | 4 | 4 | 3 | 4 | 5 | 4 | 7 | 4 | 73 |
| £15,907 | T64 | Round 3 | 4 | 4 | 4 | 4 | 5 | 4 | 4 | 3 | 4 | 4 | 2 | 3 | 4 | 4 | 3 | 6 | 5 | 3 | 70 |
| | **T58** | Round 4 | 4 | 4 | 4 | 4 | 5 | 4 | 4 | 2 | 4 | 3 | 4 | 4 | 5 | 4 | 5 | 4 | 4 | 3 | 71-**285** |
| **Gary Woodland** | T64 | Round 1 | 3 | 4 | 4 | 4 | 4 | 4 | 4 | 3 | 3 | 3 | 4 | 5 | 5 | 6 | 4 | 4 | 4 | 4 | 72 |
| USA | T39 | Round 2 | 4 | 4 | 4 | 4 | 5 | 4 | 3 | 3 | 4 | 4 | 4 | 4 | 3 | 4 | 4 | 4 | 5 | 3 | 70 |
| £15,907 | T57 | Round 3 | 3 | 4 | 4 | 3 | 4 | 4 | 5 | 3 | 4 | 3 | 4 | 4 | 4 | 5 | 4 | 4 | 5 | 4 | 71 |
| | **T58** | Round 4 | 3 | 4 | 4 | 5 | 4 | 4 | 4 | 3 | 3 | 4 | 3 | 4 | 5 | 5 | 3 | 5 | 5 | 5 | 72-**285** |
| **David Lipsky** | T87 | Round 1 | 4 | 3 | 4 | 4 | 6 | 4 | 4 | 3 | 4 | 3 | 4 | 4 | 4 | 4 | 4 | 4 | 6 | 4 | 73 |
| USA | T39 | Round 2 | 4 | 3 | 4 | 4 | 5 | 4 | 4 | 3 | 4 | 3 | 4 | 4 | 4 | 4 | 4 | 4 | 4 | 3 | 69 |
| £15,907 | T45 | Round 3 | 4 | 4 | 3 | 4 | 5 | 4 | 4 | 3 | 4 | 3 | 4 | 4 | 4 | 5 | 4 | 4 | 4 | 3 | 70 |
| | **T58** | Round 4 | 4 | 4 | 4 | 3 | 4 | 4 | 3 | 4 | 4 | 4 | 3 | 5 | 5 | 5 | 4 | 5 | 4 | 4 | 73-**285** |
| **Kevin Na** | T8 | Round 1 | 4 | 4 | 3 | 4 | 5 | 4 | 4 | 3 | 3 | 4 | 2 | 4 | 3 | 5 | 4 | 4 | 4 | 3 | 67 |
| USA | T39 | Round 2 | 5 | 5 | 4 | 5 | 4 | 6 | 4 | 3 | 3 | 4 | 2 | 4 | 5 | 4 | 5 | 4 | 5 | 3 | 75 |
| £15,907 | T45 | Round 3 | 4 | 5 | 3 | 4 | 5 | 4 | 4 | 3 | 3 | 5 | 2 | 3 | 4 | 4 | 4 | 4 | 5 | 4 | 70 |
| | **T58** | Round 4 | 4 | 4 | 3 | 5 | 5 | 4 | 3 | 3 | 4 | 4 | 3 | 5 | 3 | 5 | 4 | 4 | 5 | 5 | 73-**285** |
| **Jason Dufner** | T87 | Round 1 | 5 | 3 | 3 | 4 | 4 | 3 | 4 | 3 | 4 | 4 | 4 | 5 | 4 | 6 | 4 | 5 | 5 | 3 | 73 |
| USA | T61 | Round 2 | 3 | 4 | 3 | 5 | 4 | 4 | 4 | 3 | 4 | 3 | 4 | 5 | 4 | 4 | 4 | 4 | 6 | 3 | 71 |
| £15,907 | T33 | Round 3 | 4 | 3 | 4 | 5 | 4 | 3 | 4 | 3 | 4 | 3 | 4 | 3 | 4 | 4 | 4 | 4 | 4 | 3 | 67 |
| | **T58** | Round 4 | 4 | 5 | 5 | 4 | 4 | 4 | 3 | 4 | 3 | 3 | 4 | 4 | 7 | 4 | 4 | 5 | 4 | 3 | 74-**285** |
| **Greg Chalmers** | T24 | Round 1 | 3 | 4 | 3 | 5 | 5 | 4 | 3 | 3 | 4 | 2 | 3 | 4 | 5 | 5 | 4 | 5 | 4 | 4 | 70 |
| Australia | T25 | Round 2 | 4 | 3 | 3 | 5 | 4 | 5 | 5 | 4 | 3 | 3 | 3 | 4 | 4 | 5 | 4 | 4 | 4 | 4 | 71 |
| £15,907 | T26 | Round 3 | 4 | 4 | 3 | 4 | 5 | 3 | 4 | 3 | 4 | 3 | 3 | 4 | 4 | 5 | 4 | 4 | 4 | 4 | 69 |
| | **T58** | Round 4 | 4 | 4 | 4 | 4 | 3 | 4 | 4 | 4 | 4 | 5 | 3 | 4 | 5 | 5 | 5 | 5 | 5 | 3 | 75-**285** |
| **Thongchai Jaidee** | T64 | Round 1 | 4 | 4 | 4 | 4 | 4 | 3 | 4 | 3 | 4 | 4 | 4 | 5 | 4 | 6 | 4 | 4 | 4 | 3 | 72 |
| Thailand | T50 | Round 2 | 4 | 4 | 4 | 4 | 4 | 3 | 4 | 4 | 4 | 4 | 4 | 5 | 5 | 4 | 4 | 4 | 3 | 3 | 71 |
| £15,350 | T57 | Round 3 | 3 | 4 | 4 | 4 | 5 | 5 | 4 | 3 | 3 | 4 | 3 | 4 | 4 | 4 | 4 | 4 | 4 | 4 | 70 |
| | **T65** | Round 4 | 4 | 5 | 4 | 4 | 5 | 4 | 4 | 3 | 3 | 3 | 3 | 4 | 4 | 5 | 5 | 5 | 4 | 4 | 73-**286** |
| **Ernie Els** | T41 | Round 1 | 4 | 4 | 3 | 4 | 6 | 4 | 4 | 3 | 4 | 3 | 4 | 4 | 4 | 4 | 4 | 4 | 4 | 4 | 71 |
| South Africa | T61 | Round 2 | 4 | 4 | 4 | 4 | 4 | 5 | 4 | 4 | 3 | 4 | 4 | 4 | 4 | 5 | 4 | 4 | 4 | 4 | 73 |
| £15,350 | T57 | Round 3 | 3 | 4 | 4 | 5 | 4 | 4 | 4 | 3 | 4 | 3 | 3 | 4 | 5 | 4 | 4 | 4 | 4 | 3 | 69 |
| | **T65** | Round 4 | 3 | 4 | 4 | 4 | 5 | 3 | 4 | 3 | 4 | 4 | 3 | 5 | 5 | 5 | 4 | 4 | 5 | 4 | 73-**286** |
| **Romain Langasque*** | T18 | Round 1 | 4 | 3 | 4 | 5 | 4 | 4 | 4 | 3 | 4 | 4 | 3 | 3 | 4 | 5 | 3 | 3 | 5 | 4 | 69 |
| France | T25 | Round 2 | 4 | 4 | 4 | 4 | 4 | 4 | 4 | 3 | 4 | 4 | 3 | 4 | 4 | 5 | 3 | 6 | 4 | 4 | 72 |
| | T45 | Round 3 | 4 | 4 | 4 | 5 | 5 | 4 | 3 | 3 | 4 | 4 | 3 | 3 | 4 | 4 | 5 | 4 | 4 | 4 | 71 |
| | **T65** | Round 4 | 4 | 4 | 4 | 4 | 4 | 4 | 4 | 3 | 4 | 4 | 3 | 4 | 6 | 5 | 4 | 4 | 6 | 3 | 74-**286** |
| **Ross Fisher** | T41 | Round 1 | 4 | 5 | 3 | 4 | 4 | 4 | 3 | 3 | 4 | 4 | 3 | 4 | 5 | 4 | 5 | 5 | 4 | 3 | 71 |
| England | T61 | Round 2 | 4 | 4 | 4 | 4 | 5 | 4 | 4 | 3 | 4 | 4 | 4 | 4 | 4 | 5 | 4 | 4 | 4 | 4 | 73 |
| £14,950 | T74 | Round 3 | 4 | 6 | 5 | 3 | 4 | 4 | 4 | 3 | 4 | 4 | 2 | 4 | 4 | 5 | 5 | 4 | 4 | 3 | 72 |
| | **T68** | Round 4 | 4 | 4 | 3 | 4 | 4 | 4 | 3 | 3 | 3 | 4 | 4 | 3 | 5 | 5 | 4 | 5 | 5 | 4 | 71-**287** |

| HOLE | | | 1 | 2 | 3 | 4 | 5 | 6 | 7 | 8 | 9 | 10 | 11 | 12 | 13 | 14 | 15 | 16 | 17 | 18 | |
|---|---|---|---|---|---|---|---|---|---|---|---|---|---|---|---|---|---|---|---|---|---|
| PAR | POSITION | | 4 | 4 | 4 | 4 | 5 | 4 | 4 | 3 | 4 | 4 | 3 | 4 | 4 | 5 | 4 | 4 | 4 | 4 | TOTAL |
| **Bernd Wiesberger** | T64 | Round 1 | 3 | 4 | 4 | 4 | 4 | 4 | 4 | 3 | 4 | 4 | 4 | 5 | 4 | 3 | 4 | 5 | 5 | | 72 |
| Austria | T61 | Round 2 | 4 | 4 | 4 | 4 | 5 | 4 | 4 | 3 | 4 | 3 | 3 | 4 | 4 | 5 | 4 | 4 | 5 | 4 | 72 |
| £14,950 | T70 | Round 3 | 4 | 4 | 4 | 4 | 5 | 4 | 3 | 3 | 3 | 4 | 4 | 4 | 4 | 4 | 5 | 5 | 3 | | 71 |
| | **T68** | Round 4 | 4 | 4 | 4 | 4 | 5 | 4 | 4 | 3 | 4 | 4 | 2 | 4 | 4 | 5 | 4 | 4 | 5 | 4 | 72-**287** |
| **Richie Ramsay** | T64 | Round 1 | 4 | 3 | 4 | 4 | 5 | 4 | 3 | 3 | 4 | 3 | 4 | 3 | 7 | 4 | 4 | 5 | 4 | | 72 |
| Scotland | T50 | Round 2 | 3 | 4 | 4 | 4 | 4 | 4 | 5 | 4 | 3 | 4 | 3 | 5 | 4 | 5 | 3 | 5 | 4 | 3 | 71 |
| £14,950 | T57 | Round 3 | 5 | 4 | 4 | 4 | 4 | 3 | 4 | 4 | 4 | 4 | 4 | 4 | 3 | 4 | 4 | 4 | 4 | 3 | 70 |
| | **T68** | Round 4 | 4 | 3 | 4 | 4 | 4 | 5 | 4 | 3 | 3 | 4 | 3 | 4 | 4 | 5 | 5 | 5 | 5 | 5 | 74-**287** |
| **Harris English** | T41 | Round 1 | 3 | 4 | 4 | 4 | 4 | 4 | 4 | 3 | 4 | 4 | 4 | 4 | 4 | 4 | 3 | 5 | 5 | | 71 |
| USA | T50 | Round 2 | 4 | 4 | 4 | 4 | 5 | 3 | 4 | 3 | 3 | 4 | 3 | 4 | 4 | 5 | 5 | 5 | 5 | 3 | 72 |
| £14,950 | T45 | Round 3 | 4 | 4 | 4 | 4 | 5 | 3 | 3 | 3 | 4 | 3 | 2 | 5 | 4 | 4 | 4 | 4 | 5 | | 69 |
| | **T68** | Round 4 | 4 | 4 | 5 | 4 | 5 | 5 | 4 | 3 | 4 | 3 | 3 | 4 | 4 | 6 | 4 | 4 | 5 | 4 | 75-**287** |
| **Graham DeLaet** | T41 | Round 1 | 4 | 4 | 4 | 4 | 5 | 3 | 4 | 3 | 3 | 4 | 3 | 4 | 4 | 4 | 4 | 5 | 5 | | 71 |
| Canada | T61 | Round 2 | 4 | 4 | 4 | 4 | 3 | 4 | 5 | 3 | 4 | 4 | 3 | 4 | 3 | 5 | 6 | 4 | 5 | 4 | 73 |
| £14,950 | T45 | Round 3 | 4 | 4 | 3 | 4 | 4 | 3 | 4 | 3 | 3 | 4 | 3 | 4 | 5 | 3 | 4 | 5 | 4 | | 68 |
| | **T68** | Round 4 | 3 | 4 | 4 | 6 | 4 | 4 | 4 | 3 | 4 | 3 | 3 | 4 | 4 | 5 | 4 | 5 | 6 | 5 | 75-**287** |
| **Charl Schwartzel** | T8 | Round 1 | 4 | 5 | 3 | 4 | 4 | 3 | 3 | 3 | 4 | 3 | 3 | 3 | 4 | 4 | 4 | 5 | 4 | | 67 |
| South Africa | T14 | Round 2 | 4 | 5 | 3 | 4 | 4 | 4 | 4 | 3 | 3 | 3 | 4 | 4 | 5 | 5 | 4 | 4 | 6 | 3 | 72 |
| £14,950 | T15 | Round 3 | 5 | 3 | 4 | 4 | 4 | 4 | 3 | 3 | 3 | 2 | 3 | 5 | 6 | 4 | 3 | 4 | 5 | | 69 |
| | **T68** | Round 4 | 4 | 4 | 5 | 5 | 4 | 4 | 4 | 3 | 5 | 4 | 3 | 5 | 5 | 7 | 4 | 4 | 5 | 4 | 79-**287** |
| **Paul Casey** | T24 | Round 1 | 4 | 4 | 4 | 5 | 4 | 3 | 4 | 3 | 4 | 3 | 3 | 4 | 5 | 5 | 3 | 4 | 4 | 4 | 70 |
| England | T25 | Round 2 | 4 | 3 | 5 | 4 | 4 | 4 | 4 | 2 | 5 | 3 | 3 | 5 | 4 | 5 | 4 | 4 | 4 | 4 | 71 |
| £14,450 | T74 | Round 3 | 4 | 4 | 4 | 4 | 6 | 4 | 3 | 3 | 4 | 4 | 4 | 3 | 6 | 4 | 6 | 4 | 4 | | 75 |
| | **T74** | Round 4 | 5 | 4 | 4 | 3 | 4 | 4 | 4 | 3 | 3 | 4 | 3 | 4 | 5 | 5 | 4 | 5 | 4 | | 72-**288** |
| **Brett Rumford** | T41 | Round 1 | 5 | 4 | 3 | 4 | 4 | 3 | 4 | 3 | 4 | 4 | 4 | 5 | 4 | 4 | 4 | 4 | 4 | | 71 |
| Australia | T39 | Round 2 | 4 | 5 | 4 | 3 | 4 | 4 | 4 | 3 | 4 | 3 | 2 | 4 | 5 | 4 | 5 | 4 | 5 | 4 | 71 |
| £14,450 | T57 | Round 3 | 4 | 4 | 4 | 4 | 4 | 4 | 3 | 4 | 4 | 2 | 4 | 3 | 7 | 4 | 4 | 4 | 4 | | 71 |
| | **T74** | Round 4 | 4 | 4 | 4 | 4 | 5 | 4 | 4 | 4 | 4 | 3 | 3 | 4 | 5 | 5 | 4 | 5 | 5 | 4 | 75-**288** |
| **David Lingmerth** | T18 | Round 1 | 3 | 3 | 3 | 3 | 5 | 3 | 3 | 3 | 3 | 4 | 4 | 4 | 6 | 5 | 4 | 6 | 3 | | 69 |
| Sweden | T25 | Round 2 | 4 | 5 | 3 | 4 | 4 | 4 | 4 | 3 | 3 | 4 | 4 | 4 | 5 | 5 | 4 | 4 | 4 | 4 | 72 |
| £14,450 | T33 | Round 3 | 4 | 5 | 4 | 4 | 4 | 4 | 3 | 4 | 4 | 3 | 3 | 4 | 4 | 4 | 4 | 4 | 4 | | 70 |
| | **T74** | Round 4 | 5 | 4 | 4 | 4 | 4 | 4 | 3 | 5 | 4 | 4 | 3 | 5 | 4 | 5 | 4 | 6 | 5 | 4 | 77-**288** |
| **Ben Martin** | T109 | Round 1 | 3 | 4 | 4 | 4 | 5 | 4 | 4 | 3 | 4 | 4 | 4 | 4 | 5 | 5 | 4 | 5 | 4 | | 74 |
| USA | T61 | Round 2 | 5 | 4 | 4 | 4 | 4 | 3 | 3 | 3 | 4 | 3 | 2 | 4 | 4 | 6 | 4 | 4 | 6 | 3 | 70 |
| £14,450 | T33 | Round 3 | 4 | 4 | 5 | 4 | 4 | 3 | 4 | 3 | 4 | 4 | 3 | 4 | 3 | 4 | 4 | 4 | 4 | | 67 |
| | **T74** | Round 4 | 4 | 4 | 5 | 4 | 5 | 4 | 5 | 3 | 3 | 3 | 3 | 5 | 7 | 4 | 5 | 5 | 5 | | 77-**288** |
| **Bernhard Langer** | T109 | Round 1 | 3 | 3 | 4 | 4 | 4 | 3 | 5 | 3 | 4 | 4 | 3 | 4 | 5 | 5 | 5 | 6 | 5 | 4 | 74 |
| Germany | T61 | Round 2 | 3 | 4 | 4 | 4 | 4 | 4 | 4 | 3 | 4 | 4 | 3 | 4 | 3 | 5 | 4 | 4 | 5 | 4 | 70 |
| £14,150 | T78 | Round 3 | 4 | 4 | 5 | 7 | 5 | 4 | 4 | 3 | 3 | 4 | 2 | 5 | 3 | 5 | 4 | 3 | 4 | 4 | 73 |
| | **T78** | Round 4 | 3 | 5 | 4 | 5 | 5 | 4 | 4 | 3 | 4 | 3 | 3 | 3 | 4 | 5 | 4 | 4 | 5 | 4 | 72-**289** |
| **Mark O'Meara** | T64 | Round 1 | 3 | 5 | 4 | 4 | 4 | 4 | 4 | 3 | 4 | 4 | 3 | 3 | 4 | 5 | 4 | 5 | 5 | 4 | 72 |
| USA | T61 | Round 2 | 3 | 3 | 4 | 4 | 5 | 5 | 4 | 2 | 4 | 4 | 4 | 4 | 5 | 4 | 4 | 4 | 4 | 4 | 72 |
| £14,150 | T70 | Round 3 | 4 | 4 | 4 | 4 | 4 | 4 | 3 | 4 | 5 | 2 | 4 | 4 | 5 | 4 | 4 | 4 | 4 | | 71 |
| | **T78** | Round 4 | 4 | 4 | 4 | 4 | 5 | 3 | 4 | 3 | 4 | 4 | 4 | 5 | 5 | 4 | 5 | 5 | 4 | | 74-**289** |
| **Thomas Aiken** | T127 | Round 1 | 4 | 5 | 4 | 4 | 4 | 4 | 4 | 3 | 5 | 4 | 3 | 5 | 4 | 5 | 4 | 4 | 5 | 4 | 75 |
| South Africa | T61 | Round 2 | 4 | 4 | 4 | 4 | 5 | 4 | 4 | 3 | 4 | 3 | 3 | 5 | 4 | 4 | 4 | 4 | 3 | 3 | 69 |
| £14,000 | T74 | Round 3 | 4 | 5 | 4 | 4 | 4 | 4 | 3 | 4 | 4 | 3 | 4 | 4 | 5 | 3 | 5 | 4 | 4 | | 72 |
| | **80** | Round 4 | 4 | 4 | 4 | 5 | 4 | 4 | 4 | 3 | 3 | 3 | 4 | 4 | 5 | 6 | 4 | 4 | 5 | 4 | 74-**290** |

(Leading 10 professionals and ties receive £4,500 each, next 20 professionals and ties receive £3,600 each, remainder of professionals receive £3,000 each.)

| HOLE | | | 1 | 2 | 3 | 4 | 5 | 6 | 7 | 8 | 9 | 10 | 11 | 12 | 13 | 14 | 15 | 16 | 17 | 18 | |
|---|---|---|---|---|---|---|---|---|---|---|---|---|---|---|---|---|---|---|---|---|---|
| PAR | POSITION | | 4 | 4 | 4 | 4 | 5 | 4 | 4 | 3 | 4 | 4 | 3 | 4 | 4 | 5 | 4 | 4 | 4 | 4 | TOTAL |
| **Marcel Siem** | T24 | Round 1 | 4 | 3 | 4 | 4 | 5 | 3 | 3 | 3 | 4 | 4 | 3 | 4 | 4 | 5 | 4 | 4 | 5 | 4 | 70 |
| Germany | **T81** | Round 2 | 4 | 5 | 4 | 4 | 5 | 5 | 4 | 2 | 4 | 4 | 3 | 5 | 4 | 5 | 3 | 5 | 5 | 4 | 75 -**145** |
| **Pablo Larrazábal** | T139 | Round 1 | 3 | 4 | 5 | 5 | 5 | 4 | 4 | 3 | 5 | 4 | 3 | 4 | 4 | 5 | 4 | 5 | 5 | 4 | 76 |
| Spain | **T81** | Round 2 | 4 | 4 | 4 | 4 | 4 | 4 | 4 | 2 | 4 | 4 | 3 | 4 | 4 | 6 | 4 | 3 | 4 | 3 | 69 -**145** |
| **John Daly** | T41 | Round 1 | 4 | 4 | 3 | 5 | 4 | 4 | 3 | 3 | 3 | 3 | 4 | 5 | 4 | 4 | 4 | 5 | 5 | 4 | 71 |
| USA | **T81** | Round 2 | 4 | 5 | 4 | 4 | 5 | 4 | 4 | 3 | 4 | 4 | 3 | 4 | 4 | 5 | 4 | 5 | 5 | 3 | 74 -**145** |
| **Tommy Fleetwood** | T18 | Round 1 | 4 | 3 | 4 | 4 | 4 | 3 | 4 | 3 | 4 | 3 | 3 | 4 | 4 | 5 | 5 | 3 | 5 | 4 | 69 |
| England | **T81** | Round 2 | 4 | 4 | 4 | 6 | 5 | 5 | 4 | 3 | 4 | 4 | 3 | 4 | 4 | 5 | 4 | 4 | 5 | 4 | 76 -**145** |
| **Rikard Karlberg** | T24 | Round 1 | 4 | 4 | 3 | 4 | 4 | 3 | 4 | 3 | 4 | 3 | 3 | 4 | 4 | 5 | 4 | 5 | 4 | 5 | 70 |
| Sweden | **T81** | Round 2 | 4 | 4 | 5 | 5 | 4 | 4 | 5 | 2 | 4 | 4 | 4 | 4 | 4 | 5 | 4 | 4 | 5 | 4 | 75 -**145** |
| **Brian Harman** | T87 | Round 1 | 4 | 4 | 3 | 4 | 5 | 4 | 3 | 3 | 4 | 4 | 5 | 4 | 4 | 5 | 5 | 4 | 4 | 4 | 73 |
| USA | **T81** | Round 2 | 4 | 4 | 4 | 5 | 6 | 4 | 4 | 2 | 4 | 4 | 3 | 4 | 4 | 5 | 3 | 4 | 4 | 4 | 72 -**145** |
| **Alexander Levy** | T24 | Round 1 | 4 | 3 | 4 | 3 | 5 | 4 | 3 | 4 | 3 | 4 | 2 | 4 | 4 | 5 | 5 | 4 | 5 | 4 | 70 |
| France | **T81** | Round 2 | 6 | 4 | 4 | 4 | 4 | 4 | 4 | 3 | 5 | 4 | 3 | 5 | 4 | 6 | 4 | 4 | 4 | 3 | 75 -**145** |
| **Shane Lowry** | T87 | Round 1 | 5 | 4 | 4 | 5 | 5 | 4 | 3 | 3 | 3 | 3 | 3 | 4 | 3 | 4 | 4 | 4 | 8 | 4 | 73 |
| Republic of Ireland | **T81** | Round 2 | 4 | 4 | 4 | 4 | 5 | 4 | 4 | 3 | 4 | 3 | 4 | 4 | 4 | 5 | 4 | 4 | 4 | 4 | 72 -**145** |
| **Carl Pettersson** | T64 | Round 1 | 4 | 4 | 3 | 5 | 5 | 3 | 3 | 3 | 3 | 3 | 2 | 4 | 5 | 6 | 4 | 5 | 6 | 4 | 72 |
| Sweden | **T81** | Round 2 | 5 | 4 | 3 | 3 | 5 | 4 | 4 | 4 | 4 | 4 | 4 | 4 | 4 | 5 | 4 | 4 | 4 | 4 | 73 -**145** |
| **Victor Dubuisson** | T109 | Round 1 | 4 | 5 | 3 | 4 | 4 | 4 | 4 | 3 | 4 | 5 | 3 | 5 | 4 | 6 | 4 | 4 | 4 | 4 | 74 |
| France | **T81** | Round 2 | 5 | 4 | 4 | 4 | 4 | 4 | 4 | 3 | 4 | 4 | 3 | 4 | 4 | 3 | 5 | 5 | 3 | | 71 -**145** |
| **Kevin Kisner** | T41 | Round 1 | 3 | 4 | 3 | 4 | 4 | 4 | 4 | 3 | 4 | 4 | 5 | 4 | 5 | 5 | 4 | 4 | 4 | 3 | 71 |
| USA | **T81** | Round 2 | 5 | 4 | 4 | 4 | 4 | 4 | 4 | 3 | 4 | 4 | 4 | 4 | 4 | 6 | 4 | 4 | 5 | 3 | 74 -**145** |
| **Mikko Ilonen** | T127 | Round 1 | 5 | 5 | 4 | 5 | 5 | 3 | 4 | 3 | 4 | 3 | 3 | 4 | 4 | 5 | 5 | 5 | 4 | 4 | 75 |
| Finland | **T81** | Round 2 | 4 | 4 | 4 | 4 | 5 | 4 | 3 | 3 | 4 | 4 | 4 | 4 | 4 | 4 | 4 | 4 | 4 | 3 | 70 -**145** |
| **Jonas Blixt** | T127 | Round 1 | 4 | 5 | 4 | 4 | 4 | 4 | 4 | 3 | 4 | 4 | 3 | 5 | 4 | 5 | 4 | 5 | 5 | 4 | 75 |
| Sweden | **T93** | Round 2 | 4 | 4 | 4 | 4 | 4 | 4 | 3 | 3 | 4 | 4 | 4 | 4 | 5 | 4 | 4 | 4 | 4 | 4 | 71 -**146** |
| **Hiroyuki Fujita** | T41 | Round 1 | 4 | 3 | 4 | 4 | 4 | 4 | 4 | 3 | 4 | 4 | 4 | 4 | 4 | 6 | 4 | 4 | 4 | 4 | 71 |
| Japan | **T93** | Round 2 | 5 | 4 | 4 | 4 | 5 | 4 | 4 | 3 | 4 | 4 | 4 | 5 | 6 | 3 | 4 | 4 | 4 | | 75 -**146** |
| **Stephen Gallacher** | T87 | Round 1 | 3 | 4 | 3 | 4 | 4 | 4 | 4 | 4 | 4 | 3 | 4 | 5 | 6 | 4 | 4 | 5 | 4 | | 73 |
| Scotland | **T93** | Round 2 | 4 | 4 | 4 | 4 | 5 | 4 | 4 | 3 | 5 | 2 | 4 | 5 | 5 | 4 | 5 | 4 | 3 | | 73 -**146** |
| **Pelle Edberg** | T64 | Round 1 | 4 | 5 | 3 | 4 | 5 | 3 | 5 | 3 | 4 | 4 | 4 | 3 | 5 | 4 | 4 | 4 | 4 | 4 | 72 |
| Sweden | **T93** | Round 2 | 5 | 3 | 4 | 4 | 4 | 4 | 4 | 3 | 4 | 5 | 4 | 4 | 5 | 4 | 4 | 5 | 4 | | 74 -**146** |
| **Russell Knox** | T64 | Round 1 | 3 | 4 | 4 | 4 | 5 | 4 | 5 | 3 | 4 | 3 | 4 | 4 | 5 | 4 | 4 | 6 | 3 | | 72 |
| Scotland | **T93** | Round 2 | 4 | 4 | 5 | 4 | 4 | 5 | 4 | 3 | 4 | 3 | 3 | 5 | 4 | 5 | 4 | 5 | 4 | 4 | 74 -**146** |
| **Joost Luiten** | T109 | Round 1 | 4 | 4 | 4 | 4 | 5 | 4 | 4 | 3 | 4 | 5 | 3 | 5 | 4 | 5 | 4 | 4 | 4 | 4 | 74 |
| Netherlands | **T93** | Round 2 | 3 | 5 | 4 | 4 | 5 | 4 | 4 | 3 | 4 | 4 | 4 | 4 | 4 | 3 | 5 | 4 | 4 | | 72 -**146** |
| **Byeong-Hun An** | T109 | Round 1 | 5 | 4 | 4 | 4 | 4 | 5 | 2 | 4 | 3 | 4 | 6 | 5 | 4 | 4 | 5 | 4 | | 74 |
| Korea | **T93** | Round 2 | 5 | 4 | 4 | 4 | 4 | 4 | 3 | 4 | 4 | 3 | 5 | 3 | 5 | 4 | 4 | 5 | 3 | | 72 -**146** |
| **Brandt Snedeker** | T87 | Round 1 | 4 | 4 | 4 | 4 | 4 | 4 | 4 | 3 | 4 | 4 | 3 | 5 | 4 | 5 | 4 | 4 | 5 | 4 | 73 |
| USA | **T93** | Round 2 | 4 | 5 | 3 | 5 | 5 | 4 | 4 | 3 | 4 | 3 | 3 | 4 | 5 | 4 | 4 | 4 | 6 | 3 | 73 -**146** |
| **Darren Clarke** | T87 | Round 1 | 3 | 4 | 3 | 4 | 5 | 4 | 5 | 3 | 4 | 4 | 4 | 3 | 4 | 6 | 4 | 5 | 4 | 4 | 73 |
| Northern Ireland | **T93** | Round 2 | 4 | 4 | 4 | 4 | 5 | 4 | 3 | 2 | 4 | 4 | 3 | 4 | 4 | 5 | 5 | 6 | 5 | 3 | 73 -**146** |

| HOLE | | | 1 | 2 | 3 | 4 | 5 | 6 | 7 | 8 | 9 | 10 | 11 | 12 | 13 | 14 | 15 | 16 | 17 | 18 | |
|------|---|---|---|---|---|---|---|---|---|---|---|----|----|----|----|----|----|----|----|----|---|
| **PAR** | POSITION | | 4 | 4 | 4 | 4 | 5 | 4 | 4 | 3 | 4 | 4 | 3 | 4 | 4 | 5 | 4 | 4 | 4 | 4 | TOTAL |
| **Matteo Manassero** Italy | T87 / **T93** | Round 1 | 4 | 4 | 4 | 5 | 4 | 3 | 3 | 3 | 3 | 3 | 3 | 4 | 4 | 6 | 5 | 4 | 7 | 4 | 73 |
| | | Round 2 | 4 | 4 | 4 | 4 | 4 | 5 | 3 | 3 | 4 | 4 | 3 | 4 | 4 | 6 | 4 | 4 | 5 | 4 | 73 -**146** |
| **Raphaël Jacquelin** France | T139 / **T93** | Round 1 | 3 | 4 | 5 | 5 | 6 | 4 | 4 | 2 | 4 | 4 | 4 | 4 | 5 | 5 | 4 | 4 | 5 | 4 | 76 |
| | | Round 2 | 4 | 4 | 4 | 4 | 4 | 3 | 4 | 3 | 4 | 5 | 3 | 3 | 4 | 4 | 5 | 4 | 5 | 3 | 70 -**146** |
| **Paul Kinnear*** England | T24 / **T93** | Round 1 | 3 | 4 | 3 | 4 | 5 | 4 | 3 | 2 | 3 | 4 | 2 | 4 | 5 | 5 | 4 | 5 | 6 | 4 | 70 |
| | | Round 2 | 4 | 5 | 4 | 4 | 5 | 4 | 5 | 3 | 4 | 5 | 4 | 4 | 4 | 5 | 3 | 4 | 5 | 4 | 76 -**146** |
| **Tyrrell Hatton** England | T24 / **T93** | Round 1 | 4 | 4 | 4 | 4 | 4 | 3 | 2 | 5 | 3 | 2 | 5 | 3 | 5 | 4 | 4 | 4 | 6 | 4 | 70 |
| | | Round 2 | 5 | 4 | 5 | 5 | 4 | 4 | 4 | 3 | 4 | 4 | 3 | 5 | 6 | 6 | 4 | 3 | 4 | 3 | 76 -**146** |
| **Scott Hend** Australia | T109 / **T93** | Round 1 | 4 | 4 | 4 | 5 | 4 | 3 | 3 | 3 | 4 | 4 | 3 | 3 | 4 | 6 | 4 | 4 | 5 | 5 | 74 |
| | | Round 2 | 3 | 5 | 3 | 5 | 4 | 4 | 4 | 5 | 4 | 4 | 4 | 4 | 4 | 4 | 4 | 4 | 4 | 3 | 72 -**146** |
| **Danny Lee** New Zealand | T87 / **T107** | Round 1 | 4 | 5 | 4 | 5 | 4 | 3 | 4 | 3 | 4 | 4 | 2 | 4 | 4 | 5 | 5 | 4 | 4 | 5 | 73 |
| | | Round 2 | 4 | 4 | 4 | 4 | 5 | 4 | 3 | 3 | 4 | 4 | 3 | 4 | 4 | 5 | 4 | 7 | 5 | 3 | 74 -**147** |
| **George Coetzee** South Africa | T109 / **T107** | Round 1 | 4 | 4 | 3 | 4 | 4 | 3 | 4 | 4 | 4 | 4 | 3 | 4 | 4 | 7 | 5 | 4 | 4 | 5 | 74 |
| | | Round 2 | 4 | 4 | 4 | 3 | 5 | 3 | 3 | 4 | 4 | 4 | 3 | 4 | 4 | 6 | 5 | 4 | 6 | 3 | 73 -**147** |
| **Ryan Moore** USA | T109 / **T107** | Round 1 | 4 | 4 | 4 | 5 | 4 | 4 | 3 | 4 | 4 | 4 | 3 | 4 | 6 | 5 | 4 | 3 | 5 | 4 | 74 |
| | | Round 2 | 3 | 4 | 4 | 4 | 5 | 4 | 4 | 3 | 5 | 3 | 4 | 3 | 5 | 5 | 4 | 4 | 4 | 3 | 73 -**147** |
| **Keegan Bradley** USA | T127 / **T107** | Round 1 | 4 | 4 | 5 | 4 | 5 | 4 | 4 | 3 | 4 | 3 | 3 | 3 | 5 | 6 | 5 | 4 | 5 | 4 | 75 |
| | | Round 2 | 4 | 5 | 4 | 4 | 5 | 5 | 3 | 2 | 4 | 4 | 3 | 4 | 4 | 4 | 4 | 5 | 4 | 4 | 72 -**147** |
| **Sandy Lyle** Scotland | T41 / **T107** | Round 1 | 5 | 4 | 3 | 4 | 6 | 3 | 5 | 3 | 4 | 3 | 2 | 4 | 4 | 5 | 4 | 4 | 4 | 4 | 71 |
| | | Round 2 | 4 | 4 | 4 | 4 | 4 | 5 | 4 | 2 | 5 | 5 | 4 | 5 | 4 | 5 | 4 | 5 | 5 | 3 | 76 -**147** |
| **JB Holmes** USA | T87 / **T107** | Round 1 | 4 | 4 | 3 | 5 | 4 | 4 | 3 | 3 | 3 | 4 | 3 | 4 | 4 | 7 | 4 | 5 | 4 | 73 | |
| | | Round 2 | 4 | 5 | 3 | 4 | 5 | 4 | 4 | 3 | 3 | 5 | 3 | 6 | 4 | 4 | 5 | 4 | 4 | 4 | 74 -**147** |
| **Shinji Tomimura** Japan | T87 / **T107** | Round 1 | 3 | 4 | 5 | 5 | 5 | 4 | 3 | 3 | 4 | 4 | 2 | 4 | 5 | 4 | 4 | 5 | 5 | 73 | |
| | | Round 2 | 4 | 5 | 3 | 4 | 4 | 4 | 4 | 3 | 4 | 4 | 5 | 4 | 6 | 4 | 4 | 6 | 3 | 74 | |
| **Bubba Watson** USA | T41 / **T107** | Round 1 | 3 | 4 | 4 | 5 | 4 | 4 | 3 | 3 | 3 | 4 | 3 | 4 | 5 | 5 | 4 | 5 | 4 | 71 | |
| | | Round 2 | 4 | 5 | 5 | 4 | 5 | 4 | 4 | 3 | 4 | 4 | 3 | 4 | 5 | 4 | 3 | 5 | 7 | 3 | 76 -**147** |
| **Ian Poulter** England | T87 / **T107** | Round 1 | 4 | 4 | 5 | 4 | 5 | 4 | 3 | 4 | 3 | 3 | 4 | 5 | 5 | 4 | 4 | 4 | 4 | 73 | |
| | | Round 2 | 5 | 4 | 4 | 4 | 5 | 5 | 4 | 3 | 4 | 4 | 2 | 4 | 4 | 6 | 4 | 5 | 4 | 3 | 74 -**147** |
| **Tadahiro Takayama** Japan | T127 / **T107** | Round 1 | 4 | 4 | 3 | 4 | 6 | 3 | 4 | 3 | 4 | 5 | 3 | 4 | 5 | 5 | 5 | 4 | 4 | 5 | 75 |
| | | Round 2 | 4 | 4 | 4 | 4 | 5 | 4 | 3 | 4 | 4 | 4 | 3 | 4 | 4 | 4 | 4 | 5 | 5 | 3 | 72 -**147** |
| **David Hearn** Canada | T109 / **T107** | Round 1 | 4 | 4 | 3 | 5 | 5 | 3 | 4 | 3 | 4 | 3 | 3 | 4 | 3 | 6 | 4 | 6 | 5 | 5 | 74 |
| | | Round 2 | 4 | 4 | 4 | 5 | 5 | 4 | 4 | 3 | 4 | 5 | 3 | 5 | 4 | 4 | 4 | 3 | 4 | 4 | 73 -**147** |
| **Jaco Van Zyl** South Africa | T151 / **T118** | Round 1 | 4 | 4 | 4 | 4 | 4 | 4 | 4 | 3 | 4 | 4 | 3 | 4 | 7 | 7 | 6 | 4 | 5 | 4 | 79 |
| | | Round 2 | 3 | 4 | 4 | 5 | 4 | 4 | 3 | 5 | 4 | 4 | 3 | 3 | 4 | 4 | 4 | 4 | 3 | 4 | 69 -**148** |
| **Søren Kjeldsen** Denmark | T127 / **T118** | Round 1 | 4 | 4 | 4 | 5 | 6 | 3 | 3 | 3 | 3 | 4 | 4 | 4 | 5 | 5 | 5 | 5 | 4 | 75 | |
| | | Round 2 | 4 | 5 | 5 | 3 | 4 | 4 | 4 | 3 | 4 | 5 | 3 | 4 | 5 | 5 | 3 | 4 | 5 | 3 | 73 -**148** |
| **Miguel A Jiménez** Spain | T127 / **T118** | Round 1 | 4 | 4 | 4 | 5 | 3 | 4 | 4 | 3 | 4 | 4 | 3 | 4 | 5 | 5 | 5 | 5 | 5 | 3 | 75 |
| | | Round 2 | 4 | 4 | 4 | 4 | 4 | 4 | 2 | 4 | 4 | 4 | 5 | 4 | 6 | 4 | 4 | 4 | 4 | 73 | |
| **Tom Lehman** USA | T127 / **T118** | Round 1 | 4 | 4 | 4 | 4 | 4 | 3 | 4 | 3 | 4 | 4 | 4 | 3 | 7 | 5 | 4 | 4 | 5 | 5 | 75 |
| | | Round 2 | 3 | 3 | 3 | 5 | 5 | 4 | 5 | 3 | 4 | 4 | 4 | 4 | 5 | 5 | 4 | 4 | 5 | 3 | 73 -**148** |
| **Yuta Ikeda** Japan | T109 / **T118** | Round 1 | 4 | 4 | 5 | 4 | 3 | 3 | 4 | 3 | 4 | 4 | 4 | 4 | 7 | 4 | 4 | 5 | 4 | 74 | |
| | | Round 2 | 4 | 5 | 4 | 4 | 4 | 4 | 4 | 4 | 4 | 3 | 5 | 4 | 4 | 5 | 4 | 4 | 4 | 74 | |
| **Kiradech Aphibarnrat** Thailand | T87 / **T118** | Round 1 | 3 | 4 | 5 | 4 | 4 | 4 | 5 | 3 | 5 | 3 | 3 | 4 | 5 | 4 | 6 | 3 | 4 | 4 | 73 |
| | | Round 2 | 4 | 4 | 4 | 4 | 5 | 4 | 3 | 2 | 5 | 4 | 4 | 5 | 4 | 6 | 4 | 4 | 5 | 4 | 75 -**148** |
| **Romain Wattel** France | T127 / **T118** | Round 1 | 3 | 3 | 4 | 4 | 5 | 4 | 4 | 4 | 4 | 4 | 2 | 4 | 5 | 6 | 4 | 5 | 6 | 4 | 75 |
| | | Round 2 | 4 | 4 | 4 | 5 | 4 | 3 | 3 | 3 | 4 | 5 | 4 | 4 | 5 | 5 | 3 | 5 | 5 | 3 | 73 -**148** |

| HOLE | | | 1 | 2 | 3 | 4 | 5 | 6 | 7 | 8 | 9 | 10 | 11 | 12 | 13 | 14 | 15 | 16 | 17 | 18 | |
|---|---|---|---|---|---|---|---|---|---|---|---|---|---|---|---|---|---|---|---|---|---|
| PAR | POSITION | | 4 | 4 | 4 | 4 | 5 | 4 | 4 | 3 | 4 | 4 | 3 | 4 | 4 | 5 | 4 | 4 | 4 | 4 | TOTAL |
| **Mark Young** | T109 | Round 1 | 4 | 4 | 4 | 5 | 4 | 3 | 4 | 2 | 5 | 4 | 3 | 4 | 5 | 5 | 4 | 5 | 5 | 4 | 74 |
| England | **T118** | Round 2 | 4 | 4 | 4 | 5 | 5 | 4 | 3 | 3 | 4 | 3 | 4 | 4 | 4 | 6 | 4 | 5 | 4 | 4 | 74 **-148** |
| **James Hahn** | T127 | Round 1 | 4 | 4 | 3 | 6 | 6 | 4 | 4 | 2 | 4 | 5 | 3 | 4 | 4 | 6 | 4 | 4 | 4 | 4 | 75 |
| USA | **T118** | Round 2 | 4 | 4 | 4 | 5 | 5 | 4 | 4 | 3 | 4 | 4 | 3 | 5 | 4 | 4 | 4 | 4 | 4 | 4 | 73 **-148** |
| **Morgan Hoffmann** | T87 | Round 1 | 3 | 6 | 4 | 4 | 5 | 3 | 4 | 2 | 4 | 4 | 3 | 4 | 4 | 6 | 4 | 4 | 5 | 4 | 73 |
| USA | T127 | Round 2 | 4 | 4 | 4 | 4 | 5 | 4 | 4 | 3 | 3 | 5 | 5 | 4 | 4 | 4 | 4 | 7 | 5 | 3 | 76 **-149** |
| **Hiroshi Iwata** | T151 | Round 1 | 5 | 5 | 4 | 5 | 4 | 3 | 3 | 3 | 4 | 4 | 4 | 6 | 5 | 6 | 5 | 3 | 6 | 4 | 79 |
| Japan | T127 | Round 2 | 4 | 5 | 4 | 3 | 3 | 3 | 4 | 3 | 4 | 4 | 3 | 4 | 4 | 5 | 5 | 4 | 4 | 4 | 70 **-149** |
| **Bill Haas** | T127 | Round 1 | 3 | 4 | 3 | 5 | 6 | 4 | 3 | 3 | 4 | 4 | 3 | 4 | 4 | 5 | 5 | 4 | 7 | 4 | 75 |
| USA | T127 | Round 2 | 3 | 4 | 4 | 4 | 5 | 4 | 4 | 3 | 4 | 4 | 4 | 4 | 4 | 5 | 4 | 6 | 5 | 3 | 74 **-149** |
| **Koumei Oda** | T87 | Round 1 | 4 | 3 | 4 | 4 | 5 | 3 | 3 | 2 | 4 | 3 | 4 | 4 | 5 | 6 | 4 | 6 | 5 | 4 | 73 |
| Japan | T127 | Round 2 | 3 | 4 | 5 | 4 | 4 | 4 | 4 | 4 | 5 | 3 | 3 | 4 | 5 | 8 | 4 | 4 | 4 | 4 | 76 **-149** |
| **Edoardo Molinari** | T109 | Round 1 | 4 | 4 | 4 | 5 | 4 | 3 | 4 | 3 | 4 | 4 | 3 | 4 | 6 | 5 | 5 | 4 | 4 | 4 | 74 |
| Italy | T127 | Round 2 | 4 | 5 | 5 | 5 | 5 | 3 | 4 | 3 | 4 | 5 | 3 | 4 | 5 | 5 | 4 | 4 | 4 | 3 | 75 **-149** |
| **Daniel Berger** | T87 | Round 1 | 4 | 4 | 4 | 5 | 3 | 3 | 3 | 3 | 3 | 6 | 3 | 4 | 4 | 5 | 4 | 5 | 5 | 5 | 73 |
| USA | T127 | Round 2 | 4 | 5 | 4 | 5 | 4 | 3 | 4 | 5 | 3 | 3 | 4 | 5 | 4 | 4 | 4 | 7 | 5 | 3 | 76 **-149** |
| **Taichi Teshima** | T139 | Round 1 | 4 | 4 | 4 | 3 | 6 | 5 | 4 | 3 | 4 | 4 | 3 | 4 | 4 | 5 | 4 | 4 | 7 | 4 | 76 |
| Japan | T127 | Round 2 | 4 | 4 | 3 | 5 | 4 | 4 | 4 | 3 | 4 | 4 | 4 | 4 | 4 | 6 | 4 | 4 | 5 | 3 | 73 **-149** |
| **Thomas Bjørn** | T24 | Round 1 | 4 | 4 | 4 | 3 | 4 | 3 | 4 | 2 | 4 | 5 | 4 | 4 | 4 | 4 | 4 | 4 | 5 | 4 | 70 |
| Denmark | T127 | Round 2 | 4 | 7 | 5 | 5 | 4 | 4 | 3 | 3 | 5 | 5 | 4 | 4 | 4 | 5 | 5 | 4 | 4 | 4 | 79 **-149** |
| **Ben Curtis** | T109 | Round 1 | 4 | 4 | 4 | 4 | 4 | 5 | 4 | 3 | 4 | 4 | 3 | 4 | 5 | 5 | 4 | 4 | 5 | 4 | 74 |
| USA | T127 | Round 2 | 3 | 4 | 5 | 5 | 5 | 5 | 4 | 3 | 4 | 4 | 4 | 5 | 5 | 5 | 4 | 4 | 4 | 3 | 75 **-149** |
| **Daniel Brooks** | T139 | Round 1 | 4 | 4 | 5 | 3 | 6 | 4 | 4 | 3 | 4 | 4 | 2 | 4 | 4 | 6 | 5 | 4 | 5 | 5 | 76 |
| England | T127 | Round 2 | 4 | 4 | 3 | 5 | 6 | 4 | 4 | 3 | 4 | 5 | 1 | 4 | 5 | 4 | 5 | 4 | 4 | 4 | 73 **-149** |
| **Adam Bland** | T127 | Round 1 | 3 | 4 | 4 | 6 | 5 | 4 | 4 | 3 | 4 | 4 | 4 | 4 | 4 | 5 | 4 | 4 | 5 | 4 | 75 |
| Australia | T127 | Round 2 | 4 | 3 | 4 | 4 | 4 | 4 | 4 | 4 | 5 | 4 | 3 | 4 | 4 | 4 | 5 | 4 | 6 | 4 | 74 **-149** |
| **Liang Wen-chong** | T153 | Round 1 | 5 | 4 | 4 | 4 | 6 | 3 | 4 | 4 | 4 | 6 | 4 | 4 | 5 | 6 | 4 | 5 | 4 | 4 | 80 |
| China | **T138** | Round 2 | 4 | 4 | 5 | 4 | 4 | 2 | 3 | 2 | 4 | 4 | 4 | 4 | 5 | 5 | 4 | 4 | 5 | 3 | 70 **-150** |
| **Gunn Yang*** | T87 | Round 1 | 4 | 4 | 4 | 4 | 4 | 3 | 5 | 3 | 3 | 4 | 3 | 5 | 4 | 6 | 4 | 4 | 5 | 4 | 73 |
| Korea | **T138** | Round 2 | 4 | 4 | 5 | 4 | 4 | 4 | 4 | 3 | 4 | 5 | 3 | 6 | 5 | 6 | 4 | 4 | 5 | 3 | 77 **-150** |
| **Justin Leonard** | T149 | Round 1 | 3 | 3 | 4 | 4 | 5 | 4 | 4 | 5 | 4 | 5 | 4 | 5 | 5 | 6 | 5 | 4 | 5 | 3 | 78 |
| USA | **T138** | Round 2 | 4 | 4 | 4 | 5 | 5 | 3 | 4 | 3 | 4 | 4 | 3 | 4 | 4 | 5 | 4 | 4 | 4 | 4 | 72 **-150** |
| **Tom Gillis** | T139 | Round 1 | 5 | 4 | 3 | 5 | 4 | 4 | 4 | 3 | 4 | 4 | 3 | 4 | 4 | 6 | 4 | 6 | 5 | 4 | 76 |
| USA | **T138** | Round 2 | 3 | 5 | 4 | 4 | 5 | 3 | 4 | 4 | 3 | 3 | 4 | 4 | 4 | 5 | 5 | 5 | 5 | 4 | 74 **-150** |
| **Scott Strange** | T146 | Round 1 | 4 | 3 | 3 | 4 | 5 | 4 | 4 | 3 | 4 | 5 | 3 | 5 | 6 | 5 | 6 | 4 | 5 | 4 | 77 |
| Australia | **T138** | Round 2 | 4 | 4 | 4 | 4 | 5 | 5 | 4 | 3 | 3 | 4 | 4 | 4 | 5 | 4 | 4 | 4 | 4 | 4 | 73 **-150** |
| **Alister Balcombe*** | T109 | Round 1 | 4 | 4 | 4 | 6 | 5 | 4 | 4 | 3 | 4 | 3 | 3 | 4 | 4 | 5 | 4 | 5 | 4 | 4 | 74 |
| England | **T138** | Round 2 | 4 | 5 | 4 | 3 | 5 | 4 | 4 | 3 | 4 | 3 | 6 | 5 | 5 | 4 | 4 | 5 | 4 | 4 | 76 **-150** |
| **Robert Dinwiddie** | T87 | Round 1 | 3 | 5 | 3 | 4 | 4 | 3 | 4 | 3 | 4 | 3 | 4 | 4 | 4 | 5 | 5 | 6 | 5 | 4 | 73 |
| England | **T138** | Round 2 | 4 | 5 | 3 | 5 | 5 | 3 | 4 | 4 | 4 | 7 | 3 | 4 | 5 | 5 | 4 | 4 | 4 | 4 | 77 **-150** |
| **Charley Hoffman** | T64 | Round 1 | 4 | 4 | 3 | 4 | 5 | 4 | 3 | 3 | 5 | 3 | 3 | 3 | 4 | 6 | 4 | 4 | 6 | 4 | 72 |
| USA | **T138** | Round 2 | 4 | 5 | 6 | 4 | 5 | 6 | 4 | 3 | 4 | 4 | 4 | 4 | 4 | 4 | 5 | 4 | 5 | 3 | 78 **-150** |
| **Kevin Streelman** | T149 | Round 1 | 6 | 3 | 5 | 5 | 5 | 3 | 4 | 3 | 4 | 5 | 3 | 4 | 5 | 5 | 5 | 5 | 5 | 4 | 78 |
| USA | **T138** | Round 2 | 3 | 5 | 4 | 4 | 4 | 5 | 3 | 3 | 4 | 4 | 3 | 5 | 5 | 4 | 4 | 4 | 4 | 4 | 72 **-150** |
| **Todd Hamilton** | T109 | Round 1 | 4 | 4 | 3 | 4 | 5 | 4 | 4 | 5 | 4 | 5 | 2 | 5 | 3 | 5 | 4 | 4 | 5 | 4 | 74 |
| USA | **T147** | Round 2 | 4 | 4 | 4 | 4 | 5 | 4 | 4 | 3 | 4 | 3 | 4 | 5 | 4 | 6 | 4 | 5 | 5 | 5 | 77 **-151** |

| HOLE | | 1 | 2 | 3 | 4 | 5 | 6 | 7 | 8 | 9 | 10 | 11 | 12 | 13 | 14 | 15 | 16 | 17 | 18 | |
|---|---|---|---|---|---|---|---|---|---|---|---|---|---|---|---|---|---|---|---|---|
| PAR | POSITION | 4 | 4 | 4 | 4 | 5 | 4 | 4 | 3 | 4 | 4 | 3 | 4 | 4 | 5 | 4 | 4 | 4 | 4 | TOTAL |
| **Matt Every** | T87 Round 1 | 4 | 6 | 4 | 5 | 5 | 4 | 3 | 2 | 4 | 6 | 3 | 3 | 5 | 4 | 3 | 4 | 5 | 3 | 73 |
| USA | **T147** Round 2 | 4 | 4 | 4 | 4 | 6 | 4 | 4 | 4 | 4 | 5 | 4 | 4 | 4 | 5 | 4 | 6 | 4 | 4 | 78 **-151** |
| **Tiger Woods** | T139 Round 1 | 5 | 5 | 4 | 4 | 6 | 4 | 5 | 3 | 4 | 5 | 3 | 4 | 4 | 4 | 4 | 4 | 4 | 4 | 76 |
| USA | **T147** Round 2 | 4 | 4 | 4 | 5 | 5 | 5 | 4 | 3 | 4 | 3 | 3 | 4 | 5 | 6 | 5 | 3 | 4 | 4 | 75 **-151** |
| **Rod Pampling** | T146 Round 1 | 4 | 4 | 4 | 4 | 5 | 4 | 4 | 3 | 4 | 4 | 2 | 4 | 6 | 6 | 5 | 5 | 5 | 4 | 77 |
| Australia | **T150** Round 2 | 4 | 5 | 4 | 4 | 6 | 5 | 4 | 3 | 4 | 4 | 4 | 3 | 4 | 4 | 4 | 5 | 5 | 3 | 75 **-152** |
| **Jonathan Moore** | T109 Round 1 | 4 | 5 | 4 | 4 | 4 | 5 | 4 | 3 | 4 | 4 | 3 | 3 | 4 | 7 | 4 | 4 | 4 | 4 | 74 |
| USA | **T150** Round 2 | 4 | 5 | 6 | 5 | 5 | 5 | 5 | 3 | 4 | 4 | 4 | 4 | 5 | 4 | 4 | 4 | 4 | 3 | 78 **-152** |
| **Sir Nick Faldo** | 156 Round 1 | 5 | 4 | 4 | 5 | 5 | 5 | 5 | 3 | 5 | 5 | 3 | 4 | 5 | 8 | 4 | 4 | 5 | 4 | 83 |
| England | **152** Round 2 | 4 | 5 | 4 | 4 | 5 | 4 | 3 | 3 | 3 | 3 | 4 | 4 | 4 | 5 | 4 | 4 | 3 | 4 | 71 **-154** |
| **Mark Calcavecchia** | T153 Round 1 | 4 | 4 | 3 | 4 | 5 | 4 | 4 | 3 | 3 | 5 | 4 | 4 | 5 | 5 | 5 | 6 | 9 | 3 | 80 |
| USA | **T153** Round 2 | 5 | 4 | 4 | 5 | 4 | 4 | 4 | 3 | 4 | 4 | 2 | 4 | 4 | 6 | 5 | 5 | 5 | 3 | 75 **-155** |
| **Benjamin Taylor*** | 155 Round 1 | 4 | 4 | 4 | 4 | 5 | 4 | 4 | 3 | 5 | 4 | 3 | 5 | 5 | 6 | 4 | 6 | 8 | 4 | 82 |
| England | **T153** Round 2 | 4 | 4 | 3 | 3 | 5 | 5 | 4 | 4 | 4 | 4 | 3 | 4 | 5 | 5 | 4 | 4 | 5 | 3 | 73 **-155** |
| **Tom Watson** | T139 Round 1 | 5 | 4 | 4 | 4 | 5 | 3 | 4 | 3 | 3 | 3 | 3 | 4 | 6 | 5 | 4 | 6 | 6 | 4 | 76 |
| USA | **155** Round 2 | 5 | 4 | 4 | 5 | 5 | 5 | 4 | 3 | 4 | 3 | 5 | 4 | 6 | 5 | 5 | 5 | 5 | 5 | 80 **-156** |
| **Gary Boyd** | T146 Round 1 | 4 | 4 | 4 | 5 | 4 | 4 | 4 | 3 | 4 | 4 | 2 | 4 | 5 | 5 | 5 | 7 | 5 | 4 | 77 |
| England | **156** Round 2 | 4 | 4 | 4 | 5 | 4 | 4 | 4 | 5 | 6 | 4 | 4 | 4 | 5 | 6 | 4 | 4 | 5 | 4 | 80 **-157** |

## THE TOP TENS

### Driving Distance

1 Jason Day.....................316.9
2 Louis Oosthuizen ....... 315.9
3 Justin Rose ..................314.1
4 Brooks Koepka ...........313.8
5 Graham DeLaet ..........313.3
6 Adam Scott ................313.0
6 Gary Woodland ..........313.0
8 Branden Grace ............310.8
9 Paul Lawrie ................310.6
10 Dustin Johnson ...........310.0
60 *Zach Johnson* .............289.9

### Fairways Hit

*Maximum of 64*

1 Cameron Tringale ......... 56
1 **Thomas Aiken** ............... 56
3 *Zach Johnson* .................. 55
3 Webb Simpson.................55
3 Graham DeLaet .............55
6 Matt Jones.......................54
6 Francesco Molinari.........54
8 Anthony Wall .................53
8 Rickie Fowler..................53
8 Jamie Donaldson ............53
8 Thongchai Jaidee.............53

### Greens in Regulation

*Maximum of 72*

1 Brooks Koepka ..............64
2 Louis Oosthuizen ...........63
3 Rickie Fowler..................62
3 Bernd Wiesberger ..........62
5 Adam Scott .....................61
5 Thomas Aiken .................61
7 Jordan Spieth ..................60
7 Robert Streb ...................60
7 Billy Horschel .................60
7 Rafa Cabrera-Bello .........60
7 Cameron Tringale............60
7 David Lipsky...................60
40 *Zach Johnson* ..................55

### Putts

1 Marc Leishman.............112
2 *Zach Johnson* ..................115
2 Padraig Harrington ........115
4 Justin Rose .....................116
4 Graeme McDowell.........116
6 Luke Donald ...................117
7 Jason Day .......................118
7 Retief Goosen ................118
7 Andy Sullivan .................118
10 Greg Owen......................119
10 Phil Mickelson................119
10 Paul Lawrie ....................119
10 David Duval....................119
10 Eddie Pepperell .............119
10 Brett Rumford ...............119

# Statistical Rankings

| | Driving Distance | Rank | Fairways Hit | Rank | Greens In Regulation | Rank | Putts | Rank |
|---|---|---|---|---|---|---|---|---|
| Thomas Aiken | 290.9 | 57 | 56 | 1 | 61 | 5 | 137 | 80 |
| Scott Arnold | 300.9 | 26 | 42 | 73 | 56 | 31 | 123 | 35 |
| Steven Bowditch | 308.8 | 12 | 46 | 45 | 52 | 67 | 123 | 35 |
| Rafa Cabrera-Bello | 291.3 | 54 | 51 | 13 | 60 | 7 | 127 | 61 |
| Paul Casey | 296.6 | 35 | 47 | 38 | 53 | 59 | 126 | 56 |
| Greg Chalmers | 286.5 | 67 | 48 | 29 | 55 | 40 | 127 | 61 |
| Ashley Chesters* | 293.3 | 45 | 46 | 45 | 55 | 40 | 121 | 19 |
| Stewart Cink | 294.6 | 40 | 43 | 68 | 57 | 26 | 123 | 35 |
| Jason Day | 316.9 | 1 | 39 | 79 | 58 | 19 | 118 | 7 |
| Graham DeLaet | 313.3 | 5 | 55 | 3 | 59 | 13 | 130 | 75 |
| Luke Donald | 281.6 | 76 | 45 | 56 | 54 | 50 | 117 | 6 |
| Jamie Donaldson | 299.8 | 29 | 53 | 8 | 55 | 40 | 122 | 26 |
| Jason Dufner | 295.5 | 37 | 51 | 13 | 54 | 50 | 122 | 26 |
| Paul Dunne* | 292.9 | 46 | 48 | 29 | 55 | 40 | 121 | 19 |
| David Duval | 280.1 | 77 | 44 | 63 | 51 | 73 | 119 | 10 |
| Ernie Els | 297.8 | 33 | 47 | 38 | 52 | 67 | 123 | 35 |
| Harris English | 291.4 | 53 | 43 | 68 | 51 | 73 | 124 | 48 |
| Ross Fisher | 294.6 | 40 | 47 | 38 | 55 | 40 | 127 | 61 |
| Rickie Fowler | 299.9 | 28 | 53 | 8 | 62 | 3 | 133 | 78 |
| Ryan Fox | 296.8 | 34 | 43 | 68 | 53 | 59 | 120 | 16 |
| Marcus Fraser | 284.0 | 71 | 51 | 13 | 56 | 31 | 123 | 35 |
| Jim Furyk | 292.1 | 50 | 49 | 23 | 54 | 50 | 121 | 19 |
| Sergio Garcia | 294.1 | 44 | 43 | 68 | 59 | 13 | 123 | 35 |
| Retief Goosen | 295.6 | 36 | 48 | 29 | 49 | 78 | 118 | 7 |
| Branden Grace | 310.8 | 8 | 44 | 63 | 56 | 31 | 124 | 48 |
| Padraig Harrington | 290.3 | 58 | 39 | 79 | 51 | 73 | 115 | 2 |
| Russell Henley | 306.0 | 15 | 47 | 38 | 57 | 26 | 123 | 35 |
| Billy Horschel | 298.9 | 32 | 46 | 45 | 60 | 7 | 128 | 69 |
| David Howell | 282.3 | 75 | 46 | 45 | 56 | 31 | 124 | 48 |
| Thongchai Jaidee | 290.0 | 59 | 53 | 8 | 56 | 31 | 127 | 61 |
| Dustin Johnson | 310.0 | 10 | 43 | 53 | 53 | 59 | 124 | 48 |
| Zach Johnson | 289.9 | 60 | 55 | 3 | 55 | 40 | 115 | 2 |
| Matt Jones | 306.1 | 14 | 54 | 6 | 53 | 59 | 121 | 19 |
| Martin Kaymer | 294.6 | 40 | 50 | 18 | 58 | 19 | 123 | 35 |
| Brooks Koepka | 313.8 | 4 | 41 | 75 | 64 | 1 | 126 | 56 |
| Matt Kuchar | 292.6 | 47 | 49 | 23 | 58 | 19 | 131 | 76 |
| Anirban Lahiri | 292.4 | 49 | 45 | 56 | 54 | 50 | 121 | 19 |
| Romain Langasque* | 294.9 | 39 | 47 | 38 | 55 | 40 | 127 | 61 |
| Bernhard Langer | 282.8 | 74 | 49 | 23 | 54 | 50 | 123 | 35 |
| Paul Lawrie | 310.6 | 9 | 48 | 29 | 54 | 50 | 119 | 10 |
| Marc Leishman | 305.9 | 16 | 51 | 13 | 52 | 67 | 112 | 1 |
| David Lingmerth | 292.5 | 48 | 48 | 29 | 52 | 67 | 123 | 35 |
| David Lipsky | 291.5 | 52 | 50 | 18 | 60 | 7 | 128 | 69 |
| Hunter Mahan | 291.8 | 51 | 46 | 45 | 54 | 50 | 122 | 26 |
| Ben Martin | 286.4 | 69 | 49 | 23 | 53 | 59 | 128 | 69 |
| Hideki Matsuyama | 286.5 | 67 | 50 | 18 | 56 | 31 | 120 | 16 |
| Graeme McDowell | 286.8 | 65 | 48 | 29 | 49 | 78 | 116 | 4 |
| Phil Mickelson | 299.4 | 30 | 45 | 56 | 53 | 59 | 119 | 10 |
| Francesco Molinari | 291.1 | 55 | 54 | 6 | 53 | 59 | 121 | 19 |
| James Morrison | 285.5 | 70 | 48 | 29 | 58 | 19 | 122 | 26 |
| Kevin Na | 278.8 | 78 | 48 | 29 | 54 | 50 | 126 | 56 |
| Jordan Niebrugge* | 295.0 | 38 | 48 | 29 | 59 | 13 | 122 | 26 |
| Geoff Ogilvy | 302.1 | 22 | 44 | 63 | 55 | 40 | 124 | 48 |
| Mark O'Meara | 277.4 | 80 | 47 | 38 | 51 | 73 | 127 | 61 |
| Louis Oosthuizen | 315.9 | 2 | 49 | 23 | 63 | 2 | 123 | 35 |
| Greg Owen | 302.3 | 21 | 41 | 75 | 54 | 50 | 119 | 10 |
| Ryan Palmer | 301.3 | 24 | 46 | 45 | 55 | 40 | 122 | 26 |
| Eddie Pepperell | 302.4 | 19 | 42 | 73 | 53 | 59 | 119 | 10 |
| Richie Ramsay | 289.1 | 61 | 52 | 12 | 58 | 19 | 129 | 73 |
| Patrick Reed | 294.5 | 43 | 46 | 45 | 57 | 26 | 122 | 26 |
| Justin Rose | 314.1 | 3 | 46 | 45 | 52 | 67 | 116 | 4 |
| Brett Rumford | 286.9 | 64 | 45 | 56 | 47 | 80 | 119 | 10 |
| Oliver Schniederjans* | 308.6 | 13 | 45 | 56 | 56 | 31 | 122 | 26 |
| Charl Schwartzel | 291.0 | 56 | 41 | 75 | 52 | 67 | 123 | 35 |
| Adam Scott | 313.0 | 6 | 50 | 18 | 61 | 5 | 129 | 73 |
| John Senden | 302.6 | 18 | 51 | 13 | 55 | 40 | 124 | 48 |
| Webb Simpson | 286.8 | 65 | 55 | 3 | 58 | 19 | 127 | 61 |
| Jordan Spieth | 287.5 | 63 | 49 | 23 | 60 | 7 | 122 | 26 |
| Henrik Stenson | 301.0 | 25 | 50 | 18 | 59 | 13 | 131 | 76 |
| Robert Streb | 302.4 | 19 | 45 | 56 | 60 | 7 | 126 | 56 |
| Andy Sullivan | 288.5 | 62 | 47 | 38 | 51 | 73 | 118 | 7 |
| Brendon Todd | 278.6 | 79 | 46 | 45 | 59 | 13 | 120 | 16 |
| Cameron Tringale | 283.4 | 73 | 56 | 1 | 60 | 7 | 128 | 69 |
| Jimmy Walker | 309.5 | 11 | 44 | 63 | 59 | 13 | 127 | 61 |
| Anthony Wall | 283.9 | 72 | 53 | 8 | 57 | 26 | 121 | 19 |
| Marc Warren | 299.1 | 31 | 44 | 63 | 57 | 26 | 125 | 54 |
| Lee Westwood | 300.6 | 27 | 41 | 75 | 56 | 31 | 125 | 54 |
| Bernd Wiesberger | 301.4 | 23 | 46 | 45 | 62 | 3 | 135 | 79 |
| Danny Willett | 303.6 | 17 | 45 | 56 | 58 | 19 | 123 | 35 |
| Gary Woodland | 313.0 | 6 | 46 | 45 | 56 | 31 | 126 | 56 |

| | Driving Distance | Rank | Fairways Hit | Rank | Greens In Regulation | Rank | Putts | Rank |
|---|---|---|---|---|---|---|---|---|
| Byeong-Hun An | 296.5 | 61 | 24 | 36 | 26 | 78 | 63 | 73 |
| Kiradech Aphibarnrat | 286.8 | 113 | 16 | 155 | 26 | 78 | 65 | 104 |
| Alister Balcombe* | 297.0 | 56 | 23 | 55 | 26 | 78 | 68 | 144 |
| Daniel Berger | 295.8 | 65 | 19 | 142 | 23 | 135 | 64 | 88 |
| Thomas Bjørn | 294.5 | 75 | 21 | 107 | 23 | 135 | 62 | 59 |
| Adam Bland | 286.3 | 114 | 22 | 83 | 26 | 78 | 66 | 119 |
| Jonas Blixt | 285.5 | 118 | 27 | 9 | 26 | 78 | 66 | 119 |
| Gary Boyd | 295.0 | 71 | 22 | 83 | 23 | 135 | 68 | 144 |
| Keegan Bradley | 312.3 | 9 | 26 | 16 | 29 | 22 | 69 | 150 |
| Daniel Brooks | 281.0 | 137 | 21 | 107 | 28 | 35 | 69 | 150 |
| Mark Calcavecchia | 261.3 | 153 | 18 | 151 | 22 | 146 | 65 | 104 |
| Darren Clarke | 282.3 | 134 | 22 | 83 | 28 | 35 | 65 | 104 |
| George Coetzee | 296.5 | 61 | 24 | 36 | 25 | 102 | 64 | 88 |
| Ben Curtis | 260.0 | 155 | 20 | 133 | 23 | 135 | 64 | 88 |
| John Daly | 301.0 | 43 | 24 | 36 | 24 | 120 | 62 | 59 |
| Robert Dinwiddie | 278.5 | 141 | 22 | 83 | 22 | 146 | 62 | 59 |
| Victor Dubuisson | 290.5 | 99 | 23 | 55 | 27 | 60 | 65 | 104 |
| Pelle Edberg | 309.3 | 15 | 22 | 83 | 28 | 35 | 66 | 119 |
| Matt Every | 283.3 | 130 | 21 | 107 | 25 | 102 | 67 | 136 |
| Sir Nick Faldo | 278.8 | 140 | 27 | 9 | 23 | 135 | 67 | 136 |
| Tommy Fleetwood | 309.8 | 14 | 22 | 83 | 28 | 35 | 66 | 119 |
| Hiroyuki Fujita | 284.8 | 123 | 23 | 55 | 26 | 78 | 63 | 73 |
| Stephen Gallacher | 295.0 | 71 | 21 | 107 | 24 | 120 | 64 | 88 |
| Tom Gillis | 281.0 | 137 | 21 | 107 | 25 | 102 | 66 | 119 |
| Bill Haas | 297.0 | 56 | 25 | 25 | 24 | 120 | 62 | 59 |
| James Hahn | 294.8 | 74 | 28 | 2 | 29 | 22 | 69 | 150 |
| Todd Hamilton | 285.8 | 117 | 21 | 107 | 24 | 120 | 66 | 119 |
| Brian Harman | 308.8 | 16 | 27 | 9 | 28 | 35 | 65 | 104 |
| Tyrrell Hatton | 306.5 | 22 | 20 | 133 | 24 | 120 | 61 | 42 |
| David Hearn | 287.8 | 110 | 22 | 83 | 29 | 22 | 67 | 136 |
| Scott Hend | 304.3 | 31 | 23 | 55 | 27 | 60 | 67 | 136 |
| Charley Hoffman | 291.8 | 92 | 24 | 36 | 28 | 35 | 70 | 155 |
| Morgan Hoffmann | 283.3 | 130 | 22 | 83 | 23 | 135 | 58 | 8 |
| JB Holmes | 303.0 | 36 | 23 | 55 | 27 | 60 | 66 | 119 |
| Yuta Ikeda | 303.3 | 33 | 22 | 83 | 24 | 120 | 65 | 104 |
| Mikko Ilonen | 293.3 | 83 | 18 | 151 | 23 | 135 | 60 | 24 |
| Hiroshi Iwata | 304.8 | 28 | 21 | 107 | 23 | 135 | 61 | 42 |
| Raphaël Jacquelin | 299.8 | 48 | 26 | 16 | 24 | 120 | 61 | 42 |
| Miguel Angel Jiménez | 275.8 | 143 | 26 | 16 | 20 | 156 | 61 | 42 |
| Rikard Karlberg | 302.0 | 40 | 24 | 36 | 25 | 102 | 64 | 88 |
| Paul Kinnear* | 283.8 | 129 | 18 | 151 | 28 | 35 | 65 | 104 |
| Kevin Kisner | 308.0 | 17 | 24 | 36 | 28 | 35 | 67 | 136 |
| Søren Kjeldsen | 277.0 | 142 | 23 | 55 | 22 | 146 | 61 | 42 |
| Russell Knox | 297.0 | 56 | 20 | 133 | 29 | 22 | 69 | 150 |
| Pablo Larrazábal | 286.3 | 114 | 23 | 55 | 26 | 78 | 63 | 73 |
| Danny Lee | 283.0 | 133 | 26 | 16 | 30 | 8 | 66 | 119 |
| Tom Lehman | 288.0 | 109 | 25 | 25 | 31 | 3 | 68 | 144 |
| Justin Leonard | 292.3 | 90 | 26 | 16 | 25 | 102 | 66 | 119 |
| Alexander Levy | 288.5 | 107 | 23 | 55 | 29 | 22 | 66 | 119 |
| Liang Wen-chong | 303.3 | 33 | 23 | 55 | 27 | 60 | 69 | 150 |
| Shane Lowry | 293.0 | 86 | 23 | 55 | 30 | 8 | 64 | 88 |
| Joost Luiten | 297.3 | 54 | 25 | 25 | 30 | 8 | 68 | 144 |
| Sandy Lyle | 266.8 | 150 | 23 | 55 | 25 | 102 | 61 | 42 |
| Matteo Manassero | 251.5 | 156 | 23 | 55 | 22 | 146 | 58 | 8 |
| Edoardo Molinari | 288.5 | 107 | 19 | 142 | 24 | 120 | 65 | 104 |
| Jonathan Moore | 288.8 | 106 | 21 | 107 | 21 | 152 | 64 | 88 |
| Ryan Moore | 297.8 | 53 | 21 | 107 | 26 | 78 | 63 | 73 |
| Koumei Oda | 305.5 | 25 | 22 | 83 | 27 | 60 | 63 | 73 |
| Rod Pampling | 293.8 | 79 | 23 | 55 | 27 | 60 | 71 | 156 |
| Carl Pettersson | 290.0 | 103 | 23 | 55 | 25 | 102 | 62 | 59 |
| Ian Poulter | 270.3 | 149 | 23 | 55 | 26 | 78 | 65 | 104 |
| Marcel Siem | 311.0 | 13 | 20 | 133 | 26 | 78 | 63 | 73 |
| Brandt Snedeker | 293.3 | 83 | 24 | 36 | 28 | 35 | 66 | 119 |
| Scott Strange | 285.5 | 118 | 24 | 36 | 25 | 102 | 66 | 119 |
| Kevin Streelman | 291.5 | 93 | 19 | 142 | 23 | 135 | 62 | 59 |
| Tadahiro Takayama | 299.0 | 51 | 20 | 133 | 24 | 120 | 64 | 88 |
| Benjamin Taylor* | 296.3 | 63 | 21 | 107 | 24 | 120 | 67 | 136 |
| Taichi Teshima | 271.3 | 148 | 21 | 107 | 21 | 152 | 60 | 24 |
| Shinji Tomimura | 265.3 | 151 | 21 | 107 | 27 | 60 | 66 | 119 |
| Jaco Van Zyl | 295.5 | 66 | 24 | 36 | 28 | 35 | 63 | 73 |
| Bubba Watson | 304.3 | 31 | 20 | 133 | 28 | 35 | 65 | 104 |
| Tom Watson | 261.0 | 154 | 23 | 55 | 21 | 152 | 66 | 119 |
| Romain Wattel | 292.3 | 90 | 21 | 107 | 25 | 102 | 63 | 73 |
| Tiger Woods | 308.0 | 17 | 19 | 142 | 23 | 135 | 65 | 104 |
| Gunn Yang* | 312.8 | 8 | 20 | 133 | 21 | 152 | 62 | 59 |
| Mark Young | 290.8 | 98 | 23 | 55 | 26 | 78 | 66 | 119 |

# Roll of Honour

| Year | Champion | Score | Margin | Runners-up | Venue |
|------|----------|-------|--------|------------|-------|
| 1860 | Willie Park Sr | 174 | 2 | Tom Morris Sr | Prestwick |
| 1861 | Tom Morris Sr | 163 | 4 | Willie Park Sr | Prestwick |
| 1862 | Tom Morris Sr | 163 | 13 | Willie Park Sr | Prestwick |
| 1863 | Willie Park Sr | 168 | 2 | Tom Morris Sr | Prestwick |
| 1864 | Tom Morris Sr | 167 | 2 | Andrew Strath | Prestwick |
| 1865 | Andrew Strath | 162 | 2 | Willie Park Sr | Prestwick |
| 1866 | Willie Park Sr | 169 | 2 | David Park | Prestwick |
| 1867 | Tom Morris Sr | 170 | 2 | Willie Park Sr | Prestwick |
| 1868 | Tommy Morris Jr | 154 | 3 | Tom Morris Sr | Prestwick |
| 1869 | Tommy Morris Jr | 157 | 11 | Bob Kirk | Prestwick |
| 1870 | Tommy Morris Jr | 149 | 12 | Bob Kirk, Davie Strath | Prestwick |
| 1871 | *No Competition* | | | | |
| 1872 | Tommy Morris Jr | 166 | 3 | Davie Strath | Prestwick |
| 1873 | Tom Kidd | 179 | 1 | Jamie Anderson | St Andrews |
| 1874 | Mungo Park | 159 | 2 | Tommy Morris Jr | Musselburgh |
| 1875 | Willie Park Sr | 166 | 2 | Bob Martin | Prestwick |
| 1876 | Bob Martin | 176 | — | Davie Strath | St Andrews |
| | (Martin was awarded the title when Strath refused to play-off) | | | | |
| 1877 | Jamie Anderson | 160 | 2 | Bob Pringle | Musselburgh |
| 1878 | Jamie Anderson | 157 | 2 | Bob Kirk | Prestwick |
| 1879 | Jamie Anderson | 169 | 3 | Jamie Allan, Andrew Kirkaldy | St Andrews |
| 1880 | Bob Ferguson | 162 | 5 | Peter Paxton | Musselburgh |
| 1881 | Bob Ferguson | 170 | 3 | Jamie Anderson | Prestwick |
| 1882 | Bob Ferguson | 171 | 3 | Willie Fernie | St Andrews |
| 1883 | Willie Fernie | 158 | Play-off | Bob Ferguson | Musselburgh |
| 1884 | Jack Simpson | 160 | 4 | Douglas Rolland, Willie Fernie | Prestwick |
| 1885 | Bob Martin | 171 | 1 | Archie Simpson | St Andrews |
| 1886 | David Brown | 157 | 2 | Willie Campbell | Musselburgh |
| 1887 | Willie Park Jr | 161 | 1 | Bob Martin | Prestwick |
| 1888 | Jack Burns | 171 | 1 | David Anderson Jr, Ben Sayers | St Andrews |
| 1889 | Willie Park Jr | 155 | Play-off | Andrew Kirkaldy | Musselburgh |
| 1890 | John Ball Jr* | 164 | 3 | Willie Fernie, Archie Simpson | Prestwick |
| 1891 | Hugh Kirkaldy | 166 | 2 | Willie Fernie, Andrew Kirkaldy | St Andrews |
| | (From 1892 the competition was extended to 72 holes) | | | | |
| 1892 | Harold Hilton* | 305 | 3 | John Ball Jr*, Hugh Kirkaldy, Sandy Herd | Muirfield |
| 1893 | Willie Auchterlonie | 322 | 2 | John Laidlay* | Prestwick |

*Darren Clarke and Tiger Woods*   *Gary Player and Peter Dawson of The R&A*   *Arnold Palmer and Peter Thomson*

| Year | Champion | Score | Margin | Runners-up | Venue |
|------|----------|-------|--------|------------|-------|
| 1894 | JH Taylor | 326 | 5 | Douglas Rolland | St George's |
| 1895 | JH Taylor | 322 | 4 | Sandy Herd | St Andrews |
| 1896 | Harry Vardon | 316 | Play-off | JH Taylor | Muirfield |
| 1897 | Harold Hilton* | 314 | 1 | James Braid | Royal Liverpool |
| 1898 | Harry Vardon | 307 | 1 | Willie Park Jr | Prestwick |
| 1899 | Harry Vardon | 310 | 5 | Jack White | St George's |
| 1900 | JH Taylor | 309 | 8 | Harry Vardon | St Andrews |
| 1901 | James Braid | 309 | 3 | Harry Vardon | Muirfield |
| 1902 | Sandy Herd | 307 | 1 | Harry Vardon, James Braid | Royal Liverpool |
| 1903 | Harry Vardon | 300 | 6 | Tom Vardon | Prestwick |
| 1904 | Jack White | 296 | 1 | James Braid, JH Taylor | Royal St George's |
| 1905 | James Braid | 318 | 5 | JH Taylor, Rowland Jones | St Andrews |
| 1906 | James Braid | 300 | 4 | JH Taylor | Muirfield |
| 1907 | Arnaud Massy | 312 | 2 | JH Taylor | Royal Liverpool |
| 1908 | James Braid | 291 | 8 | Tom Ball | Prestwick |
| 1909 | JH Taylor | 295 | 6 | James Braid, Tom Ball | Cinque Ports |
| 1910 | James Braid | 299 | 4 | Sandy Herd | St Andrews |
| 1911 | Harry Vardon | 303 | Play-off | Arnaud Massy | Royal St George's |
| 1912 | Ted Ray | 295 | 4 | Harry Vardon | Muirfield |
| 1913 | JH Taylor | 304 | 8 | Ted Ray | Royal Liverpool |
| 1914 | Harry Vardon | 306 | 3 | JH Taylor | Prestwick |
| *1915-1919 No Championship* | | | | | |
| 1920 | George Duncan | 303 | 2 | Sandy Herd | Cinque Ports |
| 1921 | Jock Hutchison | 296 | Play-off | Roger Wethered* | St Andrews |
| 1922 | Walter Hagen | 300 | 1 | George Duncan, Jim Barnes | Royal St George's |
| 1923 | Arthur Havers | 295 | 1 | Walter Hagen | Troon |
| 1924 | Walter Hagen | 301 | 1 | Ernest Whitcombe | Royal Liverpool |
| 1925 | Jim Barnes | 300 | 1 | Archie Compston, Ted Ray | Prestwick |
| 1926 | Bobby Jones* | 291 | 2 | Al Watrous | Royal Lytham |
| 1927 | Bobby Jones* | 285 | 6 | Aubrey Boomer, Fred Robson | St Andrews |
| 1928 | Walter Hagen | 292 | 2 | Gene Sarazen | Royal St George's |
| 1929 | Walter Hagen | 292 | 6 | Johnny Farrell | Muirfield |
| 1930 | Bobby Jones* | 291 | 2 | Leo Diegel, Macdonald Smith | Royal Liverpool |
| 1931 | Tommy Armour | 296 | 1 | Jose Jurado | Carnoustie |

| Year | Champion | Score | Margin | Runners-up | Venue |
|------|----------|-------|--------|------------|-------|
| 1932 | Gene Sarazen | 283 | 5 | Macdonald Smith | Prince's |
| 1933 | Denny Shute | 292 | Play-off | Craig Wood | St Andrews |
| 1934 | Henry Cotton | 283 | 5 | Sid Brews | Royal St George's |
| 1935 | Alf Perry | 283 | 4 | Alf Padgham | Muirfield |
| 1936 | Alf Padgham | 287 | 1 | Jimmy Adams | Royal Liverpool |
| 1937 | Henry Cotton | 290 | 2 | Reg Whitcombe | Carnoustie |
| 1938 | Reg Whitcombe | 295 | 2 | Jimmy Adams | Royal St George's |
| 1939 | Dick Burton | 290 | 2 | Johnny Bulla | St Andrews |
| 1940-1945 *No Championship* | | | | | |
| 1946 | Sam Snead | 290 | 4 | Bobby Locke, Johnny Bulla | St Andrews |
| 1947 | Fred Daly | 293 | 1 | Reg Horne, Frank Stranahan* | Royal Liverpool |
| 1948 | Henry Cotton | 284 | 5 | Fred Daly | Muirfield |
| 1949 | Bobby Locke | 283 | Play-off | Harry Bradshaw | Royal St George's |
| 1950 | Bobby Locke | 279 | 2 | Roberto de Vicenzo | Troon |
| 1951 | Max Faulkner | 285 | 2 | Antonio Cerda | Royal Portrush |
| 1952 | Bobby Locke | 287 | 1 | Peter Thomson | Royal Lytham |
| 1953 | Ben Hogan | 282 | 4 | Frank Stranahan*, Dai Rees, Peter Thomson, Antonio Cerda | Carnoustie |
| 1954 | Peter Thomson | 283 | 1 | Syd Scott, Dai Rees, Bobby Locke | Royal Birkdale |
| 1955 | Peter Thomson | 281 | 2 | John Fallon | St Andrews |
| 1956 | Peter Thomson | 286 | 3 | Flory Van Donck | Royal Liverpool |
| 1957 | Bobby Locke | 279 | 3 | Peter Thomson | St Andrews |
| 1958 | Peter Thomson | 278 | Play-off | Dave Thomas | Royal Lytham |
| 1959 | Gary Player | 284 | 2 | Flory van Donck, Fred Bullock | Muirfield |
| 1960 | Kel Nagle | 278 | 1 | Arnold Palmer | St Andrews |
| 1961 | Arnold Palmer | 284 | 1 | Dai Rees | Royal Birkdale |
| 1962 | Arnold Palmer | 276 | 6 | Kel Nagle | Troon |
| 1963 | Bob Charles | 277 | Play-off | Phil Rodgers | Royal Lytham |
| 1964 | Tony Lema | 279 | 5 | Jack Nicklaus | St Andrews |
| 1965 | Peter Thomson | 285 | 2 | Christy O'Connor Sr, Brian Huggett | Royal Birkdale |
| 1966 | Jack Nicklaus | 282 | 1 | Dave Thomas, Doug Sanders | Muirfield |
| 1967 | Roberto de Vicenzo | 278 | 2 | Jack Nicklaus | Royal Liverpool |
| 1968 | Gary Player | 289 | 2 | Jack Nicklaus, Bob Charles | Carnoustie |
| 1969 | Tony Jacklin | 280 | 2 | Bob Charles | Royal Lytham |
| 1970 | Jack Nicklaus | 283 | Play-off | Doug Sanders | St Andrews |
| 1971 | Lee Trevino | 278 | 1 | Liang Huan Lu | Royal Birkdale |
| 1972 | Lee Trevino | 278 | 1 | Jack Nicklaus | Muirfield |
| 1973 | Tom Weiskopf | 276 | 3 | Neil Coles, Johnny Miller | Troon |
| 1974 | Gary Player | 282 | 4 | Peter Oosterhuis | Royal Lytham |
| 1975 | Tom Watson | 279 | Play-off | Jack Newton | Carnoustie |
| 1976 | Johnny Miller | 279 | 6 | Jack Nicklaus, Seve Ballesteros | Royal Birkdale |
| 1977 | Tom Watson | 268 | 1 | Jack Nicklaus | Turnberry |
| 1978 | Jack Nicklaus | 281 | 2 | Simon Owen, Ben Crenshaw, Ray Floyd, Tom Kite | St Andrews |
| 1979 | Seve Ballesteros | 283 | 3 | Jack Nicklaus, Ben Crenshaw | Royal Lytham |
| 1980 | Tom Watson | 271 | 4 | Lee Trevino | Muirfield |
| 1981 | Bill Rogers | 276 | 4 | Bernhard Langer | Royal St George's |
| 1982 | Tom Watson | 284 | 1 | Peter Oosterhuis, Nick Price | Royal Troon |
| 1983 | Tom Watson | 275 | 1 | Hale Irwin, Andy Bean | Royal Birkdale |
| 1984 | Seve Ballesteros | 276 | 2 | Bernhard Langer, Tom Watson | St Andrews |
| 1985 | Sandy Lyle | 282 | 1 | Payne Stewart | Royal St George's |
| 1986 | Greg Norman | 280 | 5 | Gordon J Brand | Turnberry |
| 1987 | Nick Faldo | 279 | 1 | Rodger Davis, Paul Azinger | Muirfield |
| 1988 | Seve Ballesteros | 273 | 2 | Nick Price | Royal Lytham |

*On Tuesday 27 past Champions gathered for dinner along with George Macgregor, Captain of the Royal and Ancient Golf Club.*

| Year | Champion | Score | Margin | Runners-up | Venue |
|------|----------|-------|--------|-----------|-------|
| 1989 | Mark Calcavecchia | 275 | Play-off | Greg Norman, Wayne Grady | Royal Troon |
| 1990 | Nick Faldo | 270 | 5 | Mark McNulty, Payne Stewart | St Andrews |
| 1991 | Ian Baker-Finch | 272 | 2 | Mike Harwood | Royal Birkdale |
| 1992 | Nick Faldo | 272 | 1 | John Cook | Muirfield |
| 1993 | Greg Norman | 267 | 2 | Nick Faldo | Royal St George's |
| 1994 | Nick Price | 268 | 1 | Jesper Parnevik | Turnberry |
| 1995 | John Daly | 282 | Play-off | Costantino Rocca | St Andrews |
| 1996 | Tom Lehman | 271 | 2 | Mark McCumber, Ernie Els | Royal Lytham |
| 1997 | Justin Leonard | 272 | 3 | Jesper Parnevik, Darren Clarke | Royal Troon |
| 1998 | Mark O'Meara | 280 | Play-off | Brian Watts | Royal Birkdale |
| 1999 | Paul Lawrie | 290 | Play-off | Justin Leonard, Jean Van de Velde | Carnoustie |
| 2000 | Tiger Woods | 269 | 8 | Ernie Els, Thomas Bjørn | St Andrews |
| 2001 | David Duval | 274 | 3 | Niclas Fasth | Royal Lytham |
| 2002 | Ernie Els | 278 | Play-off | Thomas Levet, Stuart Appleby, Steve Elkington | Muirfield |
| 2003 | Ben Curtis | 283 | 1 | Thomas Bjørn, Vijay Singh | Royal St George's |
| 2004 | Todd Hamilton | 274 | Play-off | Ernie Els | Royal Troon |
| 2005 | Tiger Woods | 274 | 5 | Colin Montgomerie | St Andrews |
| 2006 | Tiger Woods | 270 | 2 | Chris DiMarco | Royal Liverpool |
| 2007 | Padraig Harrington | 277 | Play-off | Sergio Garcia | Carnoustie |
| 2008 | Padraig Harrington | 283 | 4 | Ian Poulter | Royal Birkdale |
| 2009 | Stewart Cink | 278 | Play-off | Tom Watson | Turnberry |
| 2010 | Louis Oosthuizen | 272 | 7 | Lee Westwood | St Andrews |
| 2011 | Darren Clarke | 275 | 3 | Phil Mickelson, Dustin Johnson | Royal St George's |
| 2012 | Ernie Els | 273 | 1 | Adam Scott | Royal Lytham |
| 2013 | Phil Mickelson | 281 | 3 | Henrik Stenson | Muirfield |
| 2014 | Rory McIlroy | 271 | 2 | Sergio Garcia, Rickie Fowler | Royal Liverpool |
| 2015 | Zach Johnson | 273 | Play-off | Louis Oosthuizen, Marc Leishman | St Andrews |

# Records

## Most Victories

6: Harry Vardon, 1896, 1898, 1899, 1903, 1911, 1914
5: James Braid, 1901, 1905, 1906, 1908, 1910; JH Taylor, 1894, 1895, 1900, 1909, 1913; Peter Thomson, 1954, 1955, 1956, 1958, 1965; Tom Watson, 1975, 1977, 1980, 1982, 1983

## Most Runner-Up or Joint Runner-Up Finishes

7: Jack Nicklaus, 1964, 1967, 1968, 1972, 1976, 1977, 1979
6: JH Taylor, 1896, 1904, 1905, 1906, 1907, 1914

## Oldest Winners

Tom Morris Sr, 1867, 46 years 102 days
Roberto de Vicenzo, 1967, 44 years 92 days
Harry Vardon, 1914, 44 years 41 days
Tom Morris Sr, 1864, 43 years 92 days
Phil Mickelson, 2013, 43 years 35 days
Darren Clarke, 2011, 42 years 337 days
Ernie Els, 2012, 42 years 279 days

## Youngest Winners

Tommy Morris Jr, 1868, 17 years 156 days
Tommy Morris Jr, 1869, 18 years 149 days
Tommy Morris Jr, 1870, 19 years 148 days
Willie Auchterlonie, 1893, 21 years 22 days
Tommy Morris Jr, 1872, 21 years 146 days
Seve Ballesteros, 1979, 22 years 103 days

## Known Oldest and Youngest Competitors

74 years, 11 months, 24 days: Tom Morris Sr, 1896
74 years, 4 months, 9 days: Gene Sarazen, 1976
14 years, 4 months, 25 days: Tommy Morris Jr, 1865

## Largest Margin of Victory

13 strokes, Tom Morris Sr, 1862
12 strokes, Tommy Morris Jr, 1870
11 strokes, Tommy Morris Jr, 1869
8 strokes, JH Taylor, 1900 and 1913; James Braid, 1908; Tiger Woods, 2000

## Lowest Winning Total by a Champion

267, Greg Norman, Royal St George's 1993 – 66, 68, 69, 64
268, Tom Watson, Turnberry, 1977 – 68, 70, 65, 65; Nick Price, Turnberry, 1994 – 69, 66, 67, 66
269, Tiger Woods, St Andrews, 2000 – 67, 66, 67, 69

## Lowest Total in Relation to Par Since 1963

19 under par: Tiger Woods, St Andrews, 2000 (269)
18 under par: Nick Faldo, St Andrews, 1990 (270); Tiger Woods, Royal Liverpool, 2006 (270)
17 under par: Rory McIlroy, Royal Liverpool, 2014 (271)

## Lowest Total by a Runner-Up

269: Jack Nicklaus, Turnberry, 1977 – 68, 70, 65, 66; Nick Faldo, Royal St George's, 1993   69, 63, 70, 67; Jesper Parnevik, Turnberry, 1994 – 68, 66, 68, 67

## Lowest Total by an Amateur

277: Jordan Niebrugge, St Andrews, 2015 – 67, 73, 67, 70

## Lowest Individual Round

63: Mark Hayes, second round, Turnberry, 1977; Isao Aoki, third round, Muirfield, 1980; Greg Norman, second round, Turnberry, 1986; Paul Broadhurst, third round, St Andrews, 1990; Jodie Mudd, fourth round, Royal Birkdale, 1991; Nick Faldo, second round, Royal St George's, 1993; Payne Stewart, fourth round, Royal St George's, 1993; Rory McIlroy, first round, St Andrews, 2010

## Lowest Individual Round by an Amateur

65: Tom Lewis, first round, Royal St George's, 2011

## Lowest First Round

63: Rory McIlroy, St Andrews, 2010

## Lowest Second Round

63: Mark Hayes, Turnberry, 1977; Greg Norman, Turnberry, 1986; Nick Faldo, Royal St George's, 1993

## Lowest Third Round

63: Isao Aoki, Muirfield, 1980; Paul Broadhurst, St Andrews, 1990

## Lowest Fourth Round

63: Jodie Mudd, Royal Birkdale, 1991; Payne Stewart, Royal St George's, 1993

## Lowest Score over the First 36 Holes

130: Nick Faldo, Muirfield, 1992 – 66, 64; Brandt Snedeker, Royal Lytham & St Annes, 2012 – 66, 64

## Lowest Score over the Middle 36 Holes

130: Fuzzy Zoeller, Turnberry, 1994 – 66, 64

## Lowest Score over the Final 36 Holes

130: Tom Watson, Turnberry, 1977 – 65, 65; Ian Baker-Finch, Royal Birkdale, 1991 – 64, 66; Anders Forsbrand, Turnberry, 1994 – 66, 64; Marc Leishman, St Andrews, 2015 – 64, 66

## Lowest Score over the First 54 Holes

198: Tom Lehman, Royal Lytham & St Annes, 1996 – 67, 67, 64
199: Nick Faldo, St Andrews, 1990 – 67, 65, 67; Nick Faldo, Muirfield, 1992 – 66, 64, 69; Adam Scott, Royal Lytham, 2012 – 64, 67, 68

## Lowest Score over the Final 54 Holes

199: Nick Price, Turnberry, 1994 – 66, 67, 66

## Lowest Score for Nine Holes

28: Denis Durnian, first nine, Royal Birkdale, 1983
29: Tom Haliburton, first nine, Royal Lytham & St Annes, 1963; Peter Thomson, first nine, Royal Lytham & St Annes, 1963; Tony Jacklin, first nine, St Andrews, 1970; Bill Longmuir, first nine, Royal Lytham & St Annes, 1979; David J Russell first nine, Royal Lytham & St Annes, 1988; Ian Baker-Finch, first nine, St Andrews, 1990; Paul Broadhurst, first nine, St Andrews, 1990; Ian Baker-Finch, first nine, Royal Birkdale, 1991; Paul McGinley, first nine, Royal Lytham & St Annes, 1996; Ernie Els, first nine, Muirfield, 2002; Sergio Garcia, first nine, Royal Liverpool, 2006; David Lingmerth, first nine, St Andrews, 2015

## Most Successive Victories

4: Tommy Morris Jr, 1868-72 *(No Championship in 1871)*
3: Jamie Anderson, 1877-79; Bob Ferguson, 1880-82; Peter Thomson, 1954-56
2: Tom Morris Sr, 1861-62; JH Taylor, 1894-95; Harry Vardon, 1898-99; James Braid, 1905-06; Bobby Jones, 1926-27; Walter Hagen, 1928-29; Bobby Locke, 1949-50; Arnold Palmer, 1961-62; Lee Trevino, 1971-72; Tom Watson, 1982-83; Tiger Woods, 2005-06; Padraig Harrington, 2007-08

## Amateurs Who Have Won The Open

3: Bobby Jones, Royal Lytham & St Annes, 1926; St Andrews, 1927; Royal Liverpool, 1930
2: Harold Hilton, Muirfield, 1892; Royal Liverpool, 1897
1: John Ball Jr, Prestwick, 1890

## Champions Who Won on Debut

Willie Park Sr, Prestwick, 1860; Tom Kidd, St Andrews, 1873; Mungo Park, Musselburgh, 1874; Jock Hutchison, St Andrews, 1921; Denny Shute, St Andrews, 1933; Ben Hogan, Carnoustie, 1953; Tony Lema, St Andrews, 1964; Tom Watson, Carnoustie, 1975; Ben Curtis, Royal St George's, 2003

## Greatest Interval Between First and Last Victory

19 years: JH Taylor, 1894-1913
18 years: Harry Vardon, 1896-1914
15 years: Willie Park Sr, 1860-75; Gary Player, 1959-74
14 years: Henry Cotton, 1934-48

# Attendance

| Year | Total |
|------|-------|
| 1960 | 39,563 |
| 1961 | 21,708 |
| 1962 | 37,098 |
| 1963 | 24,585 |
| 1964 | 35,954 |
| 1965 | 32,927 |
| 1966 | 40,182 |
| 1967 | 29,880 |
| 1968 | 51,819 |
| 1969 | 46,001 |
| 1970 | 81,593 |
| 1971 | 70,076 |
| 1972 | 84,746 |
| 1973 | 78,810 |
| 1974 | 92,796 |
| 1975 | 85,258 |
| 1976 | 92,021 |
| 1977 | 87,615 |
| 1978 | 125,271 |
| 1979 | 134,501 |
| 1980 | 131,610 |
| 1981 | 111,987 |
| 1982 | 133,299 |
| 1983 | 142,892 |
| 1984 | 193,126 |
| 1985 | 141,619 |
| 1986 | 134,261 |
| 1987 | 139,189 |
| 1988 | 191,334 |
| 1989 | 160,639 |
| 1990 | 208,680 |
| 1991 | 189,435 |
| 1992 | 146,427 |
| 1993 | 141,000 |
| 1994 | 128,000 |
| 1995 | 180,000 |
| 1996 | 170,000 |
| 1997 | 176,000 |
| 1998 | 195,100 |
| 1999 | 157,000 |
| 2000 | 230,000 |
| 2001 | 178,000 |
| 2002 | 161,500 |
| 2003 | 183,000 |
| 2004 | 176,000 |
| 2005 | 223,000 |
| 2006 | 230,000 |
| 2007 | 154,000 |
| 2008 | 201,500 |
| 2009 | 123,000 |
| 2010 | 201,000 |
| 2011 | 180,100 |
| 2012 | 181,300 |
| 2013 | 142,036 |
| 2014 | 202,917 |
| 2015 | 237,024 |

## Greatest Interval Between Victories

11 years: Henry Cotton, 1937-48 (*No Championship 1940-45*)
10 years: Ernie Els, 2002-12
9 years: Willie Park Sr, 1866-75; Bob Martin, 1876-85; JH Taylor, 1900-09; Gary Player, 1959-68

## Champions Who Have Won in Three Separate Decades

Harry Vardon, 1896, 1898 & 1899/1903/1911 & 1914
JH Taylor, 1894 & 1895/1900 & 1909/1913
Gary Player, 1959, 1968, 1974

## Competitors with the Most Top Five Finishes

16: JH Taylor; Jack Nicklaus

## Competitors Who Have Recorded the Most Rounds Under Par From 1963

59: Jack Nicklaus
54: Nick Faldo

## Competitors with the Most Finishes Under Par From 1963

15: Ernie Els
14: Jack Nicklaus; Nick Faldo
13: Tom Watson

## Champions Who Have Led Outright After Every Round

*72 hole Championships*
Ted Ray, 1912; Bobby Jones, 1927; Gene Sarazen, 1932; Henry Cotton, 1934; Tom Weiskopf, 1973; Tiger Woods, 2005; Rory McIlroy, 2014
*36 hole Championships*
Willie Park Sr, 1860 and 1866; Tom Morris Sr, 1862 and 1864; Tommy Morris Jr, 1869 and 1870; Mungo Park, 1874; Jamie Anderson, 1879; Bob Ferguson, 1880, 1881, 1882; Willie Fernie, 1883; Jack Simpson, 1884; Hugh Kirkaldy, 1891

## Largest Leads Since 1892

*After 18 holes:*
5 strokes: Sandy Herd, 1896
4 strokes: Harry Vardon, 1902; Jim Barnes, 1925; Christy O'Connor Jr, 1985
*After 36 holes:*
9 strokes: Henry Cotton, 1934
6 strokes: Abe Mitchell, 1920
*After 54 holes:*
10 strokes: Henry Cotton, 1934
7 strokes: Harry Vardon, 1903; Tony Lema, 1964
6 strokes: JH Taylor, 1900; James Braid, 1905; James Braid, 1908; Max Faulkner, 1951; Tom Lehman, 1996; Tiger Woods, 2000; Rory McIlroy, 2014

## Champions Who Had Four Rounds, Each Better than the One Before

Jack White, Royal St George's, 1904 – 80, 75, 72, 69
James Braid, Muirfield, 1906 – 77, 76, 74, 73
Ben Hogan, Carnoustie, 1953 – 73, 71, 70, 68
Gary Player, Muirfield, 1959 – 75, 71, 70, 68

## Same Number of Strokes in Each of the Four Rounds by a Champion

Denny Shute, St Andrews, 1933 – 73, 73, 73, 73 (excluding the play-off)

## Best 18-Hole Recovery by a Champion

George Duncan, Deal, 1920. Duncan was 13 strokes behind the leader, Abe Mitchell, after 36 holes and level with him after 54.

## Greatest Variation Between Rounds by a Champion

14 strokes: Henry Cotton, 1934, second round 65, fourth round 79
12 strokes: Henry Cotton, 1934, first round 67, fourth round 79
11 strokes: Jack White, 1904, first round 80, fourth round 69; Greg Norman, 1986, first round 74, second round 63; Greg Norman, 1986, second round 63, third round 74
10 strokes: Seve Ballesteros, 1979, second round 65, third round 75

## Greatest Variation Between Two Successive Rounds by a Champion

11 strokes: Greg Norman, 1986, first round 74, second round 63; Greg Norman, 1986, second round 63, third round 74
10 strokes: Seve Ballesteros, 1979, second round 65, third round 75

## Greatest Comeback by a Champion

*After 18 holes*
Harry Vardon, 1896, 11 strokes behind the leader
*After 36 holes*
George Duncan, 1920, 13 strokes behind the leader
*After 54 holes*
Paul Lawrie, 1999, 10 strokes behind the leader

## Champions Who Had Four Rounds Under 70

Greg Norman, Royal St George's, 1993 – 66, 68, 69, 64; Nick Price, Turnberry, 1994 – 69, 66, 67, 66; Tiger Woods, St Andrews, 2000 – 67, 66, 67, 69

## Competitors Who Failed to Win The Open Despite Having Four Rounds Under 70

Ernie Els, Royal St George's, 1993 – 68, 69, 69, 68; Jesper Parnevik, Turnberry, 1994 – 68, 66, 68, 67; Ernie Els, Royal Troon, 2004 – 69, 69, 68, 68; Rickie Fowler, Royal Liverpool, 2014 – 69, 69, 68, 67

## Lowest Final Round by a Champion

64: Greg Norman, Royal St George's, 1993
65: Tom Watson, Turnberry, 1977; Seve Ballesteros, Royal Lytham & St Annes, 1988; Justin Leonard, Royal Troon, 1997

## Worst Round by a Champion Since 1939

78: Fred Daly, third round, Royal Liverpool, 1947
76: Bobby Locke, second round, Royal St George's, 1949; Paul Lawrie, third round, Carnoustie, 1999

### Champion with the Worst Finishing Round Since 1939

75: Sam Snead, St Andrews, 1946

### Lowest Opening Round by a Champion

65: Louis Oosthuizen, St Andrews, 2010

### Most Open Championship Appearances

46: Gary Player
40: Sandy Lyle
38: Sandy Herd, Jack Nicklaus, Tom Watson
37: Nick Faldo

### Most Final Day Appearances Since 1892

32: Jack Nicklaus
31: Sandy Herd
30: JH Taylor
28: Ted Ray
27: Harry Vardon, James Braid, Nick Faldo
26: Peter Thomson, Gary Player, Tom Watson

### Most Appearances by a Champion Before His First Victory

19: Darren Clarke, 2011; Phil Mickelson, 2013
15: Nick Price, 1994
14: Sandy Herd, 1902
13: Ted Ray, 1912; Jack White, 1904; Reg Whitcombe, 1938; Mark O'Meara, 1998
11: George Duncan, 1920; Nick Faldo, 1987; Ernie Els, 2002; Stewart Cink, 2009; Zach Johnson, 2015
10: Roberto de Vicenzo, 1967; Padraig Harrington, 2007

### The Open Which Provided the Greatest Number of Rounds Under 70 Since 1946

148 rounds, Turnberry, 1994

### The Open with the Fewest Rounds Under 70 Since 1946

2 rounds, St Andrews, 1946; Royal Liverpool, 1947; Carnoustie, 1968

### Statistically Most Difficult Hole Since 1982

St Andrews, 1984, Par-4 17th, 4.79

### Longest Course in Open History

Carnoustie, 2007, 7,421 yards

### Number of Times Each Course Has Hosted The Open Championship

St Andrews, 29; Prestwick, 24; Muirfield, 16; Royal St George's, 14; Royal Liverpool, 12; Royal Lytham & St Annes, 11; Royal Birkdale, 9; Royal Troon, 8; Carnoustie, 7; Musselburgh, 6; Turnberry, 4; Royal Cinque Ports, 2; Royal Portrush and Prince's, 1

# Prize Money (£)

| Year | Total | First Prize | Year | Total | First Prize | Year | Total | First Prize | Year | Total | First Prize |
|---|---|---|---|---|---|---|---|---|---|---|---|
| 1860 | nil | nil | 1889 | 22 | 8 | 1963 | 8,500 | 1,500 | 1990 | 825,000 | 85,000 |
| 1863 | 10 | nil | 1890 | 29.50 | 13 | 1965 | 10,000 | 1,750 | 1991 | 900,000 | 90,000 |
| 1864 | 15 | 6 | 1891 | 28.50 | 10 | 1966 | 15,000 | 2,100 | 1992 | 950,000 | 95,000 |
| 1865 | 20 | 8 | 1892 | 110 | 35 | 1968 | 20,000 | 3,000 | 1993 | 1,000,000 | 100,000 |
| 1866 | 11 | 6 | 1893 | 100 | 30 | 1969 | 30,000 | 4,250 | 1994 | 1,100,000 | 110,000 |
| 1867 | 16 | 7 | 1900 | 125 | 50 | 1970 | 40,000 | 5,250 | 1995 | 1,250,000 | 125,000 |
| 1868 | 12 | 6 | 1910 | 135 | 50 | 1971 | 45,000 | 5,500 | 1996 | 1,400,000 | 200,000 |
| 1872 | unknown | 8 | 1920 | 225 | 75 | 1972 | 50,000 | 5,500 | 1997 | 1,600,000 | 250,000 |
| 1873 | unknown | 11 | 1927 | 275 | 75 | 1975 | 75,000 | 7,500 | 1998 | 1,800,000 | 300,000 |
| 1874 | 20 | 8 | 1930 | 400 | 100 | 1977 | 100,000 | 10,000 | 1999 | 2,000,000 | 350,000 |
| 1876 | 27 | 10 | 1931 | 500 | 100 | 1978 | 125,000 | 12,500 | 2000 | 2,750,000 | 500,000 |
| 1877 | 20 | 8 | 1946 | 1,000 | 150 | 1979 | 155,000 | 15,000 | 2001 | 3,300,000 | 600,000 |
| 1878 | unknown | 8 | 1949 | 1,500 | 300 | 1980 | 200,000 | 25,000 | 2002 | 3,800,000 | 700,000 |
| 1879 | 47 | 10 | 1951 | 1,700 | 300 | 1982 | 250,000 | 32,000 | 2003 | 3,900,000 | 700,000 |
| 1880 | unknown | 8 | 1953 | 2,500 | 500 | 1983 | 310,000 | 40,000 | 2004 | 4,000,000 | 720,000 |
| 1881 | 21 | 8 | 1954 | 3,500 | 750 | 1984 | 451,000 | 55,000 | 2007 | 4,200,000 | 750,000 |
| 1882 | 47.25 | 12 | 1955 | 3,750 | 1,000 | 1985 | 530,000 | 65,000 | 2010 | 4,800,000 | 850,000 |
| 1883 | 20 | 8 | 1958 | 4,850 | 1,000 | 1986 | 600,000 | 70,000 | 2011 | 5,000,000 | 900,000 |
| 1884 | 23 | 8 | 1959 | 5,000 | 1,000 | 1987 | 650,000 | 75,000 | 2013 | 5,250,000 | 945,000 |
| 1885 | 35.50 | 10 | 1960 | 7,000 | 1,250 | 1988 | 700,000 | 80,000 | 2014 | 5,400,000 | 975,000 |
| 1886 | 20 | 8 | 1961 | 8,500 | 1,400 | 1989 | 750,000 | 80,000 | 2015 | 6,300,000 | 1,150,000 |

# ST ANDREWS

## The 144TH OPEN
### Card of the Championship Course

| Hole | Par | Yards | Hole | Par | Yards |
|------|-----|-------|------|-----|-------|
| 1 | 4 | 375 | 10 | 4 | 386 |
| 2 | 4 | 452 | 11 | 3 | 174 |
| 3 | 4 | 398 | 12 | 4 | 348 |
| 4 | 4 | 480 | 13 | 4 | 465 |
| 5 | 5 | 570 | 14 | 5 | 614 |
| 6 | 4 | 414 | 15 | 4 | 455 |
| 7 | 4 | 371 | 16 | 4 | 418 |
| 8 | 3 | 174 | 17 | 4 | 495 |
| 9 | 4 | 352 | 18 | 4 | 356 |
| Out | 36 | 3,586 | In | 36 | 3,711 |
| | | | Total | 72 | 7,297 |

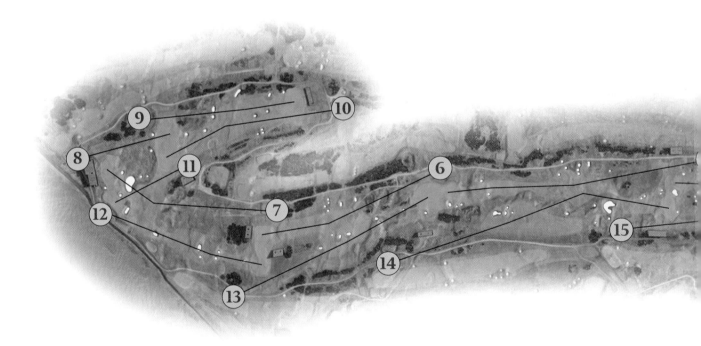